Parties and Politics in America

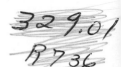

Parties and Politics
in America

———————— ⋆ ————————

CLINTON ROSSITER

CORNELL UNIVERSITY

Cornell University Press

ITHACA, NEW YORK

© 1960 by Cornell University

CORNELL UNIVERSITY PRESS

First published 1960

PRINTED IN THE UNITED STATES OF AMERICA
BY VAIL-BALLOU PRESS, INC.

To DAVID BUTLER

Friend of My Sons

Contents

Parties and Politics in America

The Pattern of American Politics

NO America without democracy, no democracy without politics, no politics without parties, no parties without compromise and moderation. So runs the string of assumptions on which hangs this exposition of the politics of American democracy.

All but the first of these are assumptions with which many Americans find it hard to live. For a people that invented the modern political party, we have been strangely reluctant to take pride in our handiwork. My modest hope is that those who come to read this book with a skeptical attitude toward party politics will go away with a better understanding of the logic of our political system, and thus perhaps with more pride in it.

Perhaps they will also go away with a hunger to read further on the subject. I can promise them happily that their stomachs will be filled. Once upon a time the vast arena in which political parties struggle ceaselessly for power, and for "place, pelf, and patronage," was called "the dark continent of political science." If it ever was dark, it is no longer. "No force acting on mankind has been less carefully examined than party," Henry Sumner Maine wrote many years ago, "and yet none better deserves examination." Were Maine alive in our America, he would be astounded by the enthusiasm and numbers of those who have taken up his challenge. Politics, whether on its institutional, functional, sociological, ideological, or psychological side, is now one of the best studied areas of American life. Thanks to the labors of dozens of distinguished scholars and journalists, the American political system is a continent surprisingly well mapped and easily traveled. If there is much that we do not know and may never know (and are probably better off not knowing) about the organization of parties and the methods of bosses and the behavior of voters, there is much that we do know, much that we can say for certain, about our politics.

This little book is an introduction to the politics of American democracy—and to the two amazing parties that hold sway over it—that draws heavily on the present stock of certainty. At the same time it does not ignore the uncertainties that continue to exist and make the whole subject worth talking about. It is intended to provide those readers who carry on to the end with a bundle of facts and opinions that may help them to find some meaningful order in the wonderful disorder of an election year—be it 1960 or any other year—in the United States. Only a small part of what I plan to say, I give warning, can be classified as gossip. I do not mean to downgrade this useful technique of a discipline that is labeled a science only by courtesy; I trust that my readers will gossip about politics, as I expect to do, for the rest of their lives. Before we can take off, however, on flights of speculation about who is going to be nominated and on what ballot, and who is going to be elected and by what margin, we must have a firm and smooth runway, and that I propose to construct by giving my readers the most objective picture I can of the present realities of American party politics. Let me begin at the beginning by calling attention to the salient characteristics of our political system.

The most momentous fact about the pattern of American politics is that we live under a persistent, obdurate, one might almost say *tyrannical,* two-party system. We have the Republicans and we have the Democrats, and we have almost no one else, no other strictly political aggregate that amounts to a corporal's guard in the struggle for power.

The extent of this tyranny of the two parties is most dramatically revealed in the sorry condition of third parties in the United States today. This may seem an odd way to begin an exposition of a two-party system, but often we can learn more about a pattern of social existence from a study of its deviants and outcasts than of its well-adjusted members. So it is with our third parties, whose present situation is almost hopeless. Whatever glories they may have known in the past, they have been faced for a generation by an almost complete monopoly of votes, attention, money, influence, and power by the two great parties. In the presidential election of 1956 a score of third-party candidates—among them Enoch Holtwick (Prohibition), Farrell Dobbs (Socialist Workers), Henry B. Krajewski (American Third Party), and T. Coleman Andrews (who ran under seven labels in nineteen states)— attracted considerably less than 1 per cent of the 62 million Americans who cast their votes. In Congress, where once Progressives, Independents, and Farmer-Laborites brightened the scene with the fireworks of nonconformity, none but Democrats and Republicans now ply their trade. In all the ninety-nine legislative chambers in the fifty states today (Nebraska is the "un-American" state with a unicameral legislature) there are exactly four men—four out of nearly 8,000 —who can be identified as adherents of a third political force.

To tell the truth, those "past glories" were not really half so glorious as some dissident romantics would like us to believe. The third parties have done their bit to keep American politics honest, principled, lively, and progressive, but it is becoming increasingly hard to nod assent to those historians, perhaps more warmhearted than cold-eyed, who have proclaimed them "the truly *dynamic* elements in our political system." There is, for example, no conclusive evidence that the third parties have been (as these writers insist) major sources of new ideas for the consideration of the American voters—and, more to the point, for eventual adoption by them. Professors Ranney and Kendall write: "The fact that a minor party can be shown to have advocated a particular reform *before* the major parties took it up . . . is no indication that the latter took it up *because* the former advocated it." [1] If we are looking for the first sources of the new ideas of the last few generations, we might look more profitably at non-party groups, like the National Municipal League, the League of Women Voters, the Anti-Saloon League, and the National Association for the Advancement of Colored People than at the Socialists, the Progressives, and even the Populists.

Six fairly distinguishable types of third party have been thrust up out of the turgid stream of American politics in the past century: [2] (1) the *left-wing splinter*, such as the Socialists, Socialist Labor party, Socialist Workers, and Communists, only the first of which ever polled more than 1 per cent of the vote in a presidential election; (2) the *one-issue obsessionists*, of whom the most durable and obsessed (and long may they thrive—as a minority, let us pray) are the Prohibitionists; (3) the *one-state party*, whether so dominant for a time that it supplants a major party (the Progressives of Wisconsin and Farmer-Labor party of Minnesota), or so vague an organizational presence that it is merely a clean tail to the soiled kite of one of the major parties (the Liberals in New York); (4) the *personal following of the dissident hero*, of which the most memorable was the Bull

Moose movement of 1912; (5) the *dissident wing of the major party*, the hastily organized band of "come-outers" with grievances that cannot for the moment be satisfied by the usual process of intraparty compromise (the Gold Democrats of 1896 and Dixiecrats of 1948); and (6) the *true minor party*, the dissident movement with the ingredients of a potential major party, of which the Populists of the late nineteenth century are the classic and perhaps only genuine example in American history. As in any attempt to be taxonomic about human groupings, we are left with several apparent sports like the La Follette Progressives of 1924 and the Wallace Progressives of 1948. These, too, can be fitted into our pattern if we classify them as hybrids of two or more of the six categories I have mentioned.

Of all the scores of minor parties that have skipped fitfully across our political landscape, only one, the Populists, seems in retrospect to have mounted a serious challenge to the hegemony of the two major parties. If ever there was a third American party that might have grown into a major party, it was this party of Ignatius Donnelly, Tom Watson, "Sockless Jerry" Simpson, and James B. Weaver. Yet the nomination of Bryan by the Democrats in 1896 smashed their dreams with one blow of the hammer, and the Populists proved how complete the wreckage was by hastening to nominate Bryan themselves.[3] Perhaps they, too, were only a dissident wing and not a genuine party. Their dissidence was momentous, to be sure, for it drove the Democrats at least five paces to the left. We are nonetheless left with the thought that the excellent showing of the Populists in 1892 meant their destruction in 1896. One of the persistent qualities of the American two-party system is the way in which one of the major parties moves almost instinctively to absorb (and thus be somewhat reshaped by) the most challenging third party of the time. In any case it is a notable fact that no third party in America has ever risen to become a major party, and that no major

party has ever fallen to become a third party. Every one of
the four great parties in American history—Federalists, Democrats, Whigs, and Republicans—sprang full-grown into the
arena and began at once to compete seriously for the stakes
of power. The two parties that died—the Federalists and
Whigs—died with few agonies and even fewer sentimental
looks back over their shoulders. It was a queer and lonely
fellow indeed who proclaimed himself a Federalist in the
Era of Good Feelings or a Whig in the Civil War. Major
parties do not decline in the United States, at least not for
long; they disappear without a trace. If the multiparty pattern
of French politics is unknown to American experience, so too,
be it noted, is the two-party pattern of British politics under
which in the course of forty years the Labour party grew
from a splinter with 29 seats in the House of Commons, to
a third party with 142, to a second party with 191, to a
majority with 288, and finally in 1945 to a crushing majority
with 394—and with a clear mandate to govern and reshape the
nation. The simultaneous slow attrition of the Liberal party
is equally without example in this country.

Third parties in the United States are not, then, especially
important in their own right, but only in terms of their influence on the major parties. We remember the Populists
because they touched off the transformation of the Democrats
in 1896, the Progressives of 1912 because they propelled
Woodrow Wilson into the Presidency, the Progressives of
1948 because they forced Harry S. Truman (to his infinite
profit) to move strongly to the left. "The evidence seems to
indicate," V. O. Key concludes,

that the rather large-scale, episodic, nonrecurring minor-party
movements must be regarded, somewhat paradoxically, as integral
elements of the so-called two-party system. They spring from the
center of the political melee and in turn they affect the nature of
the major parties and the relationships between them as they cum-
bersomely make their way from election to election.[4]

Such third parties are deviations from the norm of American two-party politics whose chief function apparently is to preserve the norm.

Another important deviation from the two-party pattern should be noted briefly. I refer to the obvious fact—not half so obvious as it was a half-century ago—of one-party dominance of many towns, cities, counties, and even states, and not alone in the Democratic South. The one-party system at the lower levels of power in the United States is essentially a phenomenon of rural politics. Samuel Lubell is the latest of a line of writers who have noted the "affinity of the small town for a one-party system." [5] The small towns are not what they used to be, yet as recently as 1956 Ranney and Kendall could argue convincingly that ten of our states—Alabama, Arkansas, Florida, Georgia, Louisiana, Mississippi, South Carolina, Texas, Vermont, Virginia—were engaged in almost pure one-party politics, and that twelve—Iowa, Kansas, Kentucky, Maine, New Hampshire, North Carolina, North Dakota, Oklahoma, Oregon, Pennsylvania, South Dakota, Tennessee—plodded along under a modified one-party system.[6] This is all very interesting and important, and one should never fail to mention it when describing our political pattern as a two-party structure; yet for us the paramount fact is that each one of the dominant parties in these twenty-two states bears the label "Republican" or "Democratic." Each one is a citadel that can withstand the impact of even the most disastrous national landslide and thus provide elements of obstinacy and stability in the two-party pattern. In short, this deviation, too, works to strengthen rather than weaken the monopoly enjoyed by the Republicans and Democrats, and thus turns out to be perhaps no deviation at all.

Many learned men have written many pages—some wise as well as learned, some merely learned—in an attempt to account conclusively for the rise and persistence of our two-party system.[7] This is, plainly, one of those grand social phenomena about whose causes we cannot ever hope to secure universal agreement, and for once we should retreat with happy consciences into the fortress of multiple causation. The two-party system got that way, let us be content to assert, because of a host of forces that group themselves conveniently under three headings:

Psychology. There is a world of substance in Maurice Duverger's insistence that "the two-party system seems to correspond to the nature of things, that is to say that political choice usually takes the form of a choice between two alternatives. A duality of parties does not always exist, but almost always there is a duality of tendencies." [8] The conditions of a freely functioning, democratic political community lead almost inevitably to a coalescing and hardening of the Ins and Outs, the Fors and Againsts, and "some other forces must intervene to produce and sustain multiparty party systems." [9]

Sociology. Those "other forces" have never been powerful enough in this country to splinter the two-party pattern for two national elections in a row. The bounty of the American economy, the fluidity of American society, the remarkable unity of principle of the American people, and, most important, the success of the American experiment have all militated against the emergence of large dissenting groups that would seek satisfaction of their special needs through the formation of political parties. Third-party politics is generally radical politics, and surely we need not rehearse once again the obvious fact that the appeals of radicalism have gone unheeded in America because the promises of radicalism have been largely fulfilled. Socialism in particular (and in all its varieties) has sailed through rough seas in this country. It foundered long ago, as Werner Sombart remarked despairingly, "on the shoals of roast beef and apple pie."

Constitutional arrangements. Most American political scientists would place particular emphasis on the bipolarizing effects of four features of our system of government: the single-member legislative district,[10] the division of power between nation and states, the method of electing a President, and the Presidency itself. The effects can be measured most graphically by imagining what might take place in our politics if we elected our legislators through a process of proportional representation, if state politics did not serve as safety valves for eccentricity and special pleading, if the general-ticket (winner-takes-all) system did not tyrannize the presidential politics of each one of the fifty states, and if the Presidency, that grandest prize in the world of politics, did not force all ambitious politicians to think and plot always in terms of building a majority.

We have more than just imaginings to lean upon in the first and fourth of these matters. Elections to the city council (then called the Board of Aldermen) in New York City in 1935 were from single-member districts. Results: Democrats, 63; Republicans, 2. In 1936 the voters of New York, having reduced the number of members, decided that it would be more sporting to try a system of proportional representation. Results of a characteristic election (1945): Democrats, 14; Republicans, 3; American Labor Party, 2; Communists, 2; Liberals, 2. Those two Communists were two too many for most persons in New York, and in 1947 the City beat a retreat to the single-member district. Results of the next election (1949): Democrats, 24; Republicans, 1—all of which proves that the single-member district system may be hard on the second party but is death on third parties.[11] As to the bipolarizing effects of a popularly chosen and powerful President, consider the lesson of the ill-starred German Republic of 1919–1933. Elections to the Reichstag were conducted under an extreme system of proportional representation, which in the election of 1930 produced a full ten parties with nineteen or more seats in the legislature as well as a wild scatter of splinter delegations. Elections to the Presidency were conducted under a system that turned the nation into one vast constituency, which in the election of 1932 forced all these scores of parties into three: two coalitions and the Communists. The two coalitions polled 90 per cent of the total popular vote of 36 million.

The two-party system will remain that way because of all the forces we have ticked off and two more that appear to be decisive: First, the whole American system of elections—electoral laws, campaign practices, social customs—is loaded heavily against the rise of minor parties to even secondary nationwide influence. The exorbitant costs of political campaigning, the statutory difficulties of getting on and staying on the ballot in many states, the legal status of the major parties as supervisors of elections—these are just a few of the roadblocks that lie in the path of any third party, no matter how strong its initial impetus or broad its purpose, that has a premonition of majority status. Second, the two-party system has become a vital principle of the American tradition. "The two-party system," C. A. Berdahl writes, "is so much a part of our governmental and political structure that it need not be argued, nor explained, nor even understood; it is, like the Constitution and the Monroe Doctrine, something we accept as a matter of course." [12]

This is the way we have always done things. This, therefore, is the way we should always do them: so runs the cast of our public mind as it contemplates the workings of American politics. There is a place in the tradition for third parties, but that place is a special one, located well out on the periphery of the system. Third parties may serve as outlets for dissent and as symbols of our vaunted tolerance, but they forget their place and invite our righteous intolerance when they thrust themselves forcefully into the struggle for power. If we cannot quite agree with J. C. Charlesworth that the two-party system "results from an act of will, on the part of men who have sensed that it is the best way to operate a republican government," [13] we can certainly agree that it is maintained by an act of will. Our will, needless to add, is itself grounded upon a firm foundation of vested interests.

The second characteristic of our system is especially striking to the eye of the student of comparative politics—the lack of ideological or programmatic commitment in both the front and rear ranks of the two major parties. One consequence is the blurring of the outer edges of each party's area of loyalty and service. Another is the deep overlapping of the beliefs and programs and even voters of the parties. They are creatures of compromise, coalitions of interest in which principle is muted and often even silenced. They are vast, gaudy, friendly umbrellas under which all Americans, whoever and wherever and however-minded they may be, are invited to stand for the sake of being counted in the next election.

The parties, moderate and tolerant and self-contradictory to a fault, are interested in the votes of men, not in their principles, and they care not at all whether the votes they gather are bestowed with passion or with indifference—so long as they are bestowed and counted. The task that they have uppermost in mind is the construction of a victorious majority, and in a country as large and diverse as ours this calls for programs and candidates having as nearly universal an appeal as the imperatives of politics will permit. It calls, that is to say, for a gallant attempt by each party to mirror the entire American electorate, an attempt that is made possible in the first place by the extraordinary unity of the people in matters of ideology. There are few places in the United States in which the Democrats and Republicans do not appeal forcefully and sincerely to every identifiable interest and group, whether economic, social, racial, religious, or even ideological. There are no interests and groups, certainly of a nationwide range, which either party is prepared to write off in advance of a national election. Our parties are noted among all parties in the world for their unforced hospitality to all manner of men. For few Americans is membership in one of our major parties taken out or renewed with zeal; the parties respond to this situation by leaving their doors wide open. It would be hard to imagine a political association more motley than the Democratic party of the United States. The Republicans, for all their apparently sterner commitment to principle and respectability, are not much less of an army with a hundred different banners. They, like the Democrats, are a vast enterprise in "group diplomacy."

Third, the structure of American politics is marked by decentralization of authority and consequent enfeebling of discipline to an exaggerated degree. Although the direction of this country's course seems to be pointed steadily toward a great magnet located somewhere in Washington—with the result that we are moving fitfully but inexorably toward more centralized, nationalized, uniform ways of doing the public business—the organizational pattern of the two major parties has thus far resisted the lure of this magnet obstinately. The Democratic and Republican parties remain today, as they have been throughout their history, loose confederacies of state parties. Each of our one hundred state parties is an independent, self-sustaining, sovereign force in the balance of political forces. It would be unthinkable for the national leadership of one of the parties, even assuming that such a locus of power exists, to dictate or veto candidates and policies of a state party. It would be impossible, too, for each state party has its own sources of influence and support that permit it to exist indefinitely in defiance of the leaders of the national party.

Each state party, in its turn, is decentralized extensively down to the city, county, town, and even precinct levels. Thanks chiefly to our federal form of government and our tradition of local self-government, the pattern of formal political organization in the United States is pluralized, dispersed, even fractured. Perhaps the best word to describe the structure of each of our two great parties is *feudal,* but it is feudalism with few enforceable pledges of faith, feudalism in which the bonds of mutual support are so loose that it often seems to border on anarchy, feudalism in which one party does not even have a king. Key puts the matter succinctly when he writes that the organization of an American party is not a "hierarchy" but "a system of layers," in which each layer—local, state, and national—is independent of the others.[14]

The top layer, moreover, is formless and powerless except for a few months in every fourth year. It is a question worth debating whether in terms of organization we have anything we can properly call "national parties" in this country. The national committees of the two parties are window-dressing bodies that meet only occasionally and resemble nothing so much as the General Assembly of the United Nations in composition, style, and power. The members of these committees are ambassadors of state parties, and they are understandably reluctant to discipline the leaders of a recalcitrant state organization for fear of setting a precedent that might be used against them. The chairmen of these committees, men of no particular consequence, are therefore defied with impunity by senators, governors, and local bosses. The absence of continuing top-level machinery for formulating party policies is notorious. The Republicans failed miserably with an Advisory Committee on Policies and Platform in the 1920's. The Democrats have done better, although not very much better, with their Advisory Council, which was set up in 1956 "to provide a collective voice for the Democratic Party." This council, like any other that might be established in the future, is indeed purely advisory, and it cannot even get Senator Johnson and Speaker Rayburn to take part in its deliberations and proclamations. All in all, one must nod sorrowful assent to E. E. Schattschneider's verdict that the organizational pattern of our parties is a kind of "truncated pyramid." Below the line, where the state and local machines operate, "authority is real." Above it, where the national committee waves its impotent scepter, "there are visible only the transparent filaments of the ghost of a party." [15]

Perhaps the most striking bit of evidence of the feeble state of national party organization is the absence from the annals of American history of politicians who, except for the special cases of two or three dominant, politically minded Presidents, can be classed as national leaders. What man, even such a man as Mark Hanna, has ever come close to being a national boss? What man, even such a man as Charles E. Hughes, has ever been able to raise his voice clearly as the spokesman of the party camped outside the White House? As Adlai Stevenson once said in his bittersweet way, could any Titular Leader be more "titular" than the defeated candidate in the most recent presidential election? Even our strong Presidents enjoyed a kind of political power that looked strong on its face but "perished in the twisting." * Think, for example, of the dramatic political ascendancy of Franklin D. Roosevelt— and of the mess he made of the Great Purge of 1938. Think, too, of Dwight D. Eisenhower and his dreams of remaking the Republican party in the image of his moderate conservatism—and of his failure to remake even one Republican who was unwilling to be remade in the first place. At the peak of his popularity, just before his crushing victory in the election of 1956, Mr. Eisenhower demonstrated his own understanding of the limits to his political power set by the organizational pattern of the Republican party. Questioned pointedly

* The other side of this coin displays the interesting fact that such political leaders as Grover Cleveland, Theodore Roosevelt, William Jennings Bryan, Woodrow Wilson, Herbert Hoover, Alfred E. Smith, Wendell Willkie, Thomas E. Dewey, and Franklin D. Roosevelt never held an official party position. They were never entitled to "participate formally in the consideration and determination of questions of party policy, strategy, management or organization." [16]

about the pose of Modern Republicanism struck by several "old guard" senators, the President replied:

Now, let's remember, there are no national parties in the United States. There are forty-eight state parties, then they are the ones that determine the people that belong to those parties. There is nothing I can do to say that no one is not a Republican. The most I can say is that in many things they do not agree with me. . . . We have got to remember that these are state organizations, and there is nothing I can do to say so-and-so is a Republican and so-and-so is not a Republican.[17]

The formal decentralization of the structure of our parties rests squarely on an informal set of "leader-follower relations of discipline and leadership" which, as Ranney and Kendall point out, "tend to be stronger at the base of the national parties' pyramids than at their top, and achieve maximum strength only at the bottom." [18] The essence of political organization is loyalty that runs in both directions, and the higher one moves up through the layers of our parties, the harder it becomes to keep such loyalty blooming with the fertilizer of personal contact.

Decentralization also rests on the notorious localism of our political attitudes. We may be a nation in most things that count—language, values, traditions, styles, goals—but not in politics, or at least not in that area of politics in which we choose candidates and elect them to office. The first test of the congressman in pursuit of re-election is his skill at running errands for the folks at home. The last hope of the congressman in danger of defeat is that "outsiders" will move in to oppose him, even or especially outsiders who belong to his party. The Republican voters of Orange and Dutchess counties in New York gave Hamilton Fish at least one extra term in the House of Representatives because he was marked out for destruction by the Modern Republicans in New York, Albany, and Washington. The air in Mississippi rings even today with the bitter wail of John Rankin, who blamed his failure to win renomination to the House in 1952 on the refusal of "Northern journalists" to "stick their noses into Mississippi" in behalf of his opponent.

The last bit of evidence one might present in illustration of this third point is the phenomenon of bossism.[19] This phenomenon, of course, is peculiarly American. There is nothing quite like a Curley or Hague or Crump or even a De Sapio in other countries that have well-developed party systems. To be a real boss, and not just a flunky, a politician must have his own base of power and immunity from external discipline, if not from internal revolt. This is exactly what our bosses have—independence. As the state bosses are independent of whatever national leadership there may be, so the local bosses are independent of them—and all are independent of one another. Regional bosses are just as unknown to our political landscape as are national bosses. The essence of the historic organizational pattern of American politics is caught in the battle cry of the Brooklyn Democrats of the 1890's as they rallied their forces to thwart another attempted invasion of their preserve by the men of Tammany: "The Tiger shall not cross the Bridge." The Tiger, more than incidentally, never did cross it.

It is a matter of some irony, and convincing proof of the point I am making, to note that the presidential nominating convention, the one truly national instrument of American politics, is little better than a happy, disorderly conclave of state and local bosses.* The many bosses have come, like the few national figures in the convention, with the common purpose of picking a winner, and they proceed toward this

* The importance of these men in the game of presidential politics is attested by the zeal with which candidates for nomination tour the country in search of their support. The road to nomination for the Presidency may lead through Washington, but it also leads through Topeka, Sacramento, Helena, Madison, Albany, and a hundred other natural habitats of state and local bosses.

goal with perhaps more unity than one might expect of them. They proceed, in any case, under their own power and at their own speed, conscious to the end of how much more important they are to the party than the party is to them. When the convention is over, they return to their principalities secure in the knowledge that their own positions of power depend only peripherally, or not at all, on the results of the presidential canvass. They will, with few exceptions, work hard for the ticket and contribute handsomely to the illusion that steals over us for four months out of every four years— that we do in fact have nationally organized parties. Yet they support their candidate for the Presidency because he heads the party's ticket and, in the nature of things political, is likely to run ahead of it in most areas—and not because he has any powers of discipline or even persuasion over them. Even in the hottest days of a presidential campaign it is plain to see that, to borrow a witticism from Stephen K. Bailey, the pattern of American politics displays "more *pluribus* than *unum.*" [20] Enthusiasm may be focused, but power remains dispersed. The imperative of organization within each of our major parties is the fragmenting of authority to the point of anarchy.

A corollary of this pattern of decentralization of political organization is the absence of common purpose, cohesion, and discipline in each of what we may call the "governmental parties," that is, in the Republican and Democratic parties as organized to govern purposefully or to oppose loyally in Congress and the state legislatures. It is an uncontested fact, documented in dozens of studies chock-full of tables and graphs, that party affiliation is only a rough index of the voting behavior of most American legislators, and no index at all in the case of some of our most interesting and powerful politicians. In some states, notably those large industrial states with developed two-party systems based on an urban-rural cleavage, there is a fair degree of party cohesion on important issues in the legislature. In others, especially in the one-party states, factions and mavericks bloom in profusion.[21] Even in Congress, where one might expect party loyalty to exercise a strong pull, the pattern of voting is so "fluid" and "unstructured" that an astute observer, James M. Burns, finds a multiparty system operating behind the two-party façade. "Instead of a grand encounter between the rallied forces of the two great parties in House and Senate," he complains with exasperation (as someone who was both an astute political scientist and a devoted party man might be expected to complain), "the legislative battle often degenerates into scuffles and skirmishes among minority groups."[22] On questions of organization, tactics, committee assignments, and distribution of patronage, the parties act with precision and regularity. On questions of taxation, veterans' benefits, farm subsidies, regulation of industry, civil rights, and defense, however, they often move as rabbles through the stages of the decision-making process. If we accept Julius Turner's definition of a party vote as one in which at least 90 per cent of the Democrats oppose 90 per cent of the Republicans,* we find that in the 1940's only 15 per cent of the roll calls in the House of Representatives were in this category. In contrast, in the days of McKinley roughly half were party votes.[23]

In a famous passage much loved and quoted by political scientists (with some reservations by this one), Schattschneider describes this characteristic of our politics:

The roll calls in the House and the Senate show that party votes are relatively rare. On difficult questions, usually the most important questions, party lines are apt to break badly, and a straight party vote, aligning one party against the other, is the exception rather than the rule. The vote is sometimes unanimous or nearly unanimous; that is, the parties are occasionally in substantial agree-

---

* In point of fact, this definition is a bit too harsh. I would settle on a figure of 75 per cent.

ment. Often both parties split into approximately equal halves. In this case the party alignment is zero. At other times one party votes as a unit but is joined by a substantial fraction of the other. Finally, a predominant portion of one party may be opposed by a predominant portion of the other party, while minorities, more or less numerous, on each side cross party lines to join their opponents. In general, the last-mentioned case is the nearest approximation to a party vote on an important issue likely to be encountered, aside from routine partisan business. . . . When all is said, it remains true that the roll calls demonstrate that *the parties are unable to hold their lines in a controversial public issue when the pressure is on.*

The condition described in the foregoing paragraph constitutes *the most important single fact concerning the American parties.* He who knows this fact, and knows nothing else, knows more about American parties than he who knows everything except this fact.[24]

The immediate cause of the lack of cohesive parties in American legislatures is the feebleness of those instruments like the caucuses and conferences that are supposed to enforce discipline in pursuit of promises made to the voting public. In this regard it is revealing to note that the few instances in which mavericks in Congress have been punished in the past half-century were touched off by actions taken not inside but outside Congress, the most obvious being the unforgivable sin of bolting the party in a presidential campaign.[25] Silence is permitted—as we learned in 1948—but only rarely active opposition to the party's candidate.

The real causes, of course, lie in the loose pattern of politics that we have been surveying, and behind them stand those forces over which, in the end, we have no real control: the diversity of American interests and the divisions in the American Constitution, which combine to permit and often even to compel the legislator to join a bipartisan bloc or to put loyalty to his favorite committee in first place or to cast nonconforming votes in behalf of interests in his constituency, and thus to compel even the fire-eaters in his party to forgive his waywardness. Indeed, the parties themselves have no choice but to be permissive—so long, that is, as they aspire to be major parties. The result, Max Beloff writes, is that "in most legislative struggles, the two parties do their best to avoid getting wholly embroiled on one side or the other and prefer to maintain official neutrality as long as possible." [26] For reasons that we shall thresh out in later chapters, this country seems destined to go on for some time to come with governmental parties—in the administrative as well as in the legislative branches—that achieve whatever cohesion they do achieve through happenstance rather than through discipline supported by an overriding sense of common principle. Let us leave this point for the time being with the observation that our system of political values makes large room for the maverick strain. Party loyalty, on issues as opposed to persons, is not one of our favorite principles. We pin the label of "hack" on the man who goes down the line. We rouse to the cry of a legislator like Senator Borah, who, when chided by a constituent for opposing the party leadership on an important issue, replied indignantly: "What would you have a Senator do? Sincerely represent his views, however inadequate they may be, or act as an intellectual prostitute for some party organization?" This is the ethos of a political system in which the pressure of party loyalty, even if the most important,[27] is only one of several kinds that work upon our decision makers in office.

While we are on the subject of pressures, let us note briefly still another unique characteristic of the American political system—the intricate web of nonparty groups that surrounds, infiltrates, and complements the two major parties.[28] There are many features that distinguish these groups from political parties, but the most important are methodological. Like the parties they try to secure the enactment and to influence the execution of public policies; unlike them they do this without nominating candidates for office, without fighting election campaigns openly and purposefully, and without seeking to gain control of government. We call them "interest groups" when we are feeling clinical, "pressure groups" when we are feeling critical, and "lobbies" when we are watching them at work in our fifty-one capitals. Whatever we call them, we are aware that they swing an inordinate amount of power for good, not-so-good, and evil over the decision makers in our legislatures, administrative branches, and—more often and influentially than we like to think—judiciaries. Parties have no monopoly on the impulse of a nation to organize politically. In all free countries men of common interests set up organizations outside of and in addition to the parties in order to grab off a larger share of whatever power, privilege, immunity, influence, and prizes there happen to be currently available. In no country does the resultant array of groups come even close to the overblown American model in terms of numbers, members, financial resources, activities, achievements, and (where the knife really cuts) persuasiveness over the minds of public men. The astounding success of the American Legion in extracting services and dollars from the Congress of the United States stands in striking contrast to the feebleness of veterans' politics in France and Britain, and this can hardly be attributed to any special feeling of generosity toward old soldiers in American hearts.

The reasons for the unique multiplicity and virility of interest groups in this country are the same as the reasons for the lack of cohesion in the governmental parties, and that lack of cohesion itself tops off all the rest. The system of values and pressures that render the legislator immune to party discipline leaves him naked and exposed, to a degree hardly comprehensible to a British parliamentarian, to the threats and appeals of those groups that have access to him—and there are some groups that have access to almost every legislator in the

land. If the party cannot discipline him, it certainly will not
support him; if it cannot punish him for disloyalty, it cannot be
expected to throw its protection around him. The American
legislator is uniquely on his own, and he lives and dies politically through the display of talents more numerous and more
demanding than party regularity. He must therefore make his
own adjustment among the forces that play upon him, even if
this means defiance of his party's leadership. We should not
feel too sorry for the exposed congressman, for this, it seems,
is the way he wants it. He may long occasionally for the
security of rigid party discipline, but on balance his life of
adventure appears to have more to offer; and he, knowing that
he cannot have it both ways, is content. Whether we should
feel sorry for ourselves, the victims of many more Indian
raids on the public treasury than we might otherwise have
suffered, is another question. Our administrators, too, feel the
pressures that arise out of this strange complex of weak parties
and strong interests. They cannot resist these pressures if they
are not protected by their masters in the legislature, and we
already know how weak the position of the masters can be.
Most administrators, so far as one can tell, would like more
security and less adventure.

I do not wish to give too exaggerated a picture of soft-
handed parties, naked congressmen, and many-splendored interest groups. Some congressmen find a large measure of independence in the very numbers of pressures that seek to force
themselves upon them, many of which cancel one another out.
Others have such a hold on their constituencies that they can
safely ignore the pressures of hostile groups. Some interest
groups are decidedly unpopular with the voters of a particular district, and congressmen may make political capital out
of a posture of defiance toward those that overreach themselves. And all congressmen, indeed all legislators throughout
the nation, learn soon enough that some of the most menacing
interest groups are so partisan, so clearly "auxiliary organiza-

tions of one or the other party," [29] that they feel no pressure from these groups at all. Either the legislator needs no persuasion to do their bidding, or they could no more persuade him than the other party could persuade him.

This tendency for interest groups to align themselves with one or the other of the major parties is a growing one, for more and more groups have found it less and less possible to remain neutral toward parties that are becoming more and more national in outlook and support. Once the process of partisan alignment has been set in motion, it propels itself along at a quickening pace. The sharpening commitment of many powerful unions to the Democratic party has forced many powerful trade associations to adopt a posture of only thinly veiled Republican partisanship. The American Legion still walks proudly down both sides of the street, dishing out plums and turnips without much concern for the politics of each recipient, but the A.F.L.-C.I.O., the U.S. Chamber of Commerce, the National Association of Manufacturers, the American Public Power Association, and even the American Farm Bureau Federation—however hotly each group may deny it—have moved a considerable distance away from "the traditional conception of pressure groups as nonpartisan organizations that pursue their objectives by building fires quite impartially under legislators of both parties." [30] They have not become slaves to one or the other party, and any one of them could and would withdraw if not switch its implicit allegiance if the party with which it now gets along comfortably were to go off in a contrary direction. Clusters of groups form about each major party because of an unforced congeniality of outlook and interest. No glue of discipline keeps them from coming unstuck and sailing back into a neutral orbit. The allegiance of most interest groups is not quite so easily given or withheld as was that of the Erie Railroad, about whose political activities Jay Gould testified candidly: "In a Republican district I was a Republican; in a Democratic district

I was a Democrat; in doubtful districts I was doubtful; but I was always Erie." [31]

Yet who can doubt that Walter Reuther is always Organized Labor, Arch N. Booth always Business, and Charles B. Shuman always Middle-Class Agrarianism? And who can deny that they are powerful allies rather than servants, on occasion even masters, of the leaders of the party with which they choose to work? The friendly groups outside each party relate to it as the factions inside the party relate to each other. The whole process of American politics appears as the give-and-take of interests in search of realization. Nowhere is the true nature of that politics more clearly revealed than in the unique tie-up of the parties and the interest groups.

In surveying the last major characteristic of American politics, we must turn our attention away from groups and toward individuals. There are several well-documented generalizations we can make about the political attitudes and behavior patterns of Americans. Together they add up to something that is, once again, unique among all democracies large and small, and we cannot hope to understand the functions, methods, and objectives of our major parties until we sense the peculiar spirit of American politics. What I am speaking of here is the absence in our behavior, as a nation and as individuals, of a deep commitment to politics as a way of living and of doing the public business. Some writers call this "apathy," others "indifference"; I prefer words like "inertia" and "offhandedness" and "resignation." In the words of this generation, which knows whereof it speaks, most Americans "play it cool" in the area of politics. Whatever words we use to describe this phenomenon, it is an evident fact that Americans give less scope to politics, are less stirred by the rhetoric of politicians, and expect less from the political process than do Frenchmen or Belgians or Italians or even Canadians. Even at the height of a presidential campaign, when the air is purple with the promises and threats of a legion of orators, the political temperature of most Americans remains low and steady.[32]

The first bit of evidence of the coolness of American politics is to be found in our attitudes toward political parties. Few Americans give to the Democrats or Republicans the deep and encompassing allegiance claimed by parties like the Socialists in Belgium and the Nationalists in South Africa. Even the loose-jointed Conservative and Labour parties of Britain look like armies of dedicated soldiers to the eye of an observer who has watched the ranks and files of the Republican and Democratic parties straggling across our political landscape. An American party is not an army, not a church, not a way of life, not even a lodge. It asks nothing of one of its adherents but his vote, a few dollars, and, if he seems willing, a few hours of his time for manning the polls, licking stamps, and ringing doorbells; and it would settle willingly for a sure vote. There is little sense of "belonging" among American voters, few signs of "shared concern" with other men of like political mind. Only a small fraction of the vast energies of the people is mobilized for party purposes. Despite the pleas of a generation of civics teachers, most Americans never perform a single act—other than registering or voting—that could be described as a service to a political party or candidate. In the course of a carefully planned study of the political activity of a cross section of 8,000 adult Americans, Julian Woodward and Elmo Roper found only 11 per cent who had "worked for election of a political candidate in the last four years," 7 per cent who had "contributed money to a party or candidate" in that span. Even by the most tolerant definition of the phrase, only one in ten of this national sample could be classed as "very active" in public affairs.[33] A study of the 1952 presidential election, surely one of the most exciting in all history, confirms these findings.

Despite the appearance of feverish public interest which characterized the 1952 campaign, it seems evident that the bulk of the political activity that went on during that period was concentrated in a fraction of perhaps one-tenth of the public. They were the meeting-goers, money-givers, party-workers. Most people took the campaign much more casually, and approximately one person in three did not seem interested enough to care which party won.[34]

The parties, well aware of the indifferent attitude most Americans have toward them and their ways, have made a peace of convenience with this state of affairs. Since they do not get, they do not really expect active demonstrations of devotion, even from the persons whose names are carried on cards in their files. They are organized to wage war in small commando units; their financial support comes principally in the form of large gifts from a few sources.[35] They do not, it appears, find this state of affairs frustrating or even disheartening. They would hardly know what to do with thousands of willing workers, and a cascade of two-dollar checks on the national committees would be almost too much trouble to cash and spend. In any case this is the state of political affairs, and it is not likely to become one whit more frantic in the foreseeable future. If Robert Michels' "iron law of oligarchy" holds sway over American politics,[36] it is at least partly because most Americans could not care less. Even the oligarchs, because of the feudal anarchy of the parties, are oligarchical only in small areas and about comparatively small things.

A related aspect of this refusal of most Americans to be politically "engaged" is the high incidence of independence. We are uniquely reluctant to acknowledge membership in a party, uniquely eager to change our minds, to cross lines, and to split tickets. Thanks to the looseness of legal definitions of party affiliation, to the fact that most of us are called upon to vote several times a year, and to the multiplicity of choices to be made in any one election, we enjoy unusual opportunities to be inconstant and even wayward; and every study made of this subject in recent years confirms the suspicion, with which our politicians must live bravely, that we seize these opportunities gaily. If ticket splitting is our privilege, ticket splitting is our delight.[37] So, too, is changing our minds from one election to the next. It has been estimated that not more than 60 per cent of the American electorate is partisan and regular in its voting habits.[38] We are seizing these opportunities, moreover, with increasing gaiety: the habit of independence is growing upon us. Issues and personalities have both become more important factors in the political calculations of American voters during the past generation. Party affiliations count a great deal less, certainly in the races for the big stakes of power at the national level. In the words of the most experienced sleuth on the American political scene, Samuel Lubell, the electorate "seems to have undergone a curious quickening of its voting reflexes" in the elections since 1948. It has become a great deal "easier to shift the party allegiance of the American voter." [39]

The chief result of this growth in independence (and of the persistence of old habits of ticket splitting) is the sight that never fails to bewilder strangers who choose to observe our antics from a safe distance: the Presidency and thus several thousand top-level executive offices safe in the hands of one party, Congress safe in the hands of the other. There is nothing in our history, to be sure, that can match the sharpness and persistence of the six-year cleavage between the Eisenhower administration and the Johnson-Rayburn Congress, yet the condition is an old one, and we have learned to live with it from years of experience. In the eighty years between 1872 and 1952, the President was faced by opposition control of one house for sixteen of those years, of both houses for eight. I do not mention this unique feature of the American system in order to defend or attack or even analyze it, but simply to call attention to the impact of independence on our ways of doing the public business. To tell the truth, it disturbs me only a little and other Americans, apparently, not at all. In any case, it is a major American political phenomenon, which might become almost the normal state of affairs in the years to come.

It is not so easy for us to take a tolerant view of what is by all odds the most striking sign of the coolness of American politics—the high, and highly troublesome, incidence of non-voting. It is well known that Americans are less disposed to exercise the precious right of suffrage (or duty or privilege, call it what you please) than just about any other nation, whether free or half-free or not free at all, in the entire world. The statistics, which in this instance are as accurate and comprehensible as voting statistics can ever be, show that the incidence of electoral participation—expressed as the percentage of voters in the potential electorate (the adult citizenry)—is:

Close to 100 per cent in totalitarian countries.

Over 90 per cent in countries having techniques of compulsory voting like Belgium and Australia.

Close to 90 per cent in Italy.

Approximately 85 per cent in West Germany.

Between 78–82 per cent in Britain, Israel, and the Scandinavian countries.

Approximately 80 per cent in France.

Approximately 75 per cent in Canada.

And, in the best showing in fifty years (1952), 64 per cent in America.

Other statistics prove that our record is both better and worse than this percentage would lead us to conclude.[40] On the credit side is the fact that, after a long dip in the graph of participation in presidential elections from 1896 to 1924, it has been inching upward painfully in recent years. The following table may serve to illustrate both the long decline, which steepened sharply in 1920 when women were first given the vote and did not know quite what to do with it, and the recent rise, which was set back noticeably in the unsettled conditions of World War II:

Year	Percentage of adult citizenry voting	Year	Percentage of adult citizenry voting
1896	79	1928	57
1900	74	1932	58
1904	66	1936	61
1908	66	1940	62
1912	60	1944	55
1916	63	1948	53
1920	49	1952	64
1924	49	1956	62

Also on the credit side is the variation in participation between the highest and lowest states. The latter are national disgraces for which we can account but make no convincing apology. The former are at least an even match for the countries with which we can be most reasonably compared—Britain, Canada, and France. Here are the high and low percentages of the 1956 election:

Idaho	80	Mississippi	22
Utah	78	South Carolina	25
Connecticut	78	Alabama	28
Massachusetts	77	Georgia	30
Rhode Island	76	Virginia	32
New Hampshire	76	Louisiana	35

To these figures should be appended the statistic that roughly 75 per cent of the electorate outside the South voted in 1952.

Lest the sight of Utah, Connecticut, and Idaho dissolve our feelings of shame, let me note that the turnout for congressional elections in off years is far below the standard we set in presidential elections. Here are some discouraging figures out of recent years:

Year	Percentage of adult citizenry voting
1946	39
1950	42
1954	43
1958	44

It is sobering to realize that in 1946, the year in which we elected our first postwar Congress, hardly one in three eligible Americans voted for their representatives. We could make even these percentages look good if we were to go into the subject of local elections, but we have enough evidence already of American apathy and inertia to satisfy us for one chapter of one small book. Let us note simply that, in defiance of the most solemn dictates of the democratic ideology, Americans lose rather than gain interest steadily as their electoral obligations move closer to home. Elections to those offices that are closest to home, where the issues are immediate and the candidates known, generally attract only a tiny percentage of the voting population. In many a village in upstate New York the turnout for the presidential election of 1956 was better than 85 per cent, in the local elections of 1955 and 1957 less than 10 per cent.

Who are the Americans who do not vote, and why don't they? Let me try to answer these questions in slightly more concrete terms than the abstract figures in which we have thus far been dealing.

In 1956 roughly 100 million Americans could conceivably have voted in the presidential election. Just over 62 million did, which means that 38 million did not. Now, according to the most generous estimate, 22.5 million could have come up with one or more of the following explanations of their failure to vote:

Six million were trapped in the political mores of the South.

For them the act of voting would have called for will power, energy, money, court assistance, or physical courage (and, in hundreds of thousands of cases, for all five) which they could not be expected to muster.

Five million (give or take a few hundred thousand—these are admittedly crude figures) were unable to meet state, county, or precinct residence requirements. They had moved too recently from one home to another, or they were men and women perpetually on the move, migrants and floaters with no permanent residence.

Five million were unable to get themselves to the polls because of illness. That may seem like a lot of sick people, but it is still only one in twenty of all adult Americans—and November is, after all, a virus-laden month.

Two and a half million were away from home, on business or "monkey business," and would not or could not use absentee ballots.

Two and a half million were unable to read and write and thus were ineligible (in 17 states) or unwilling to vote.[41]

Six hundred thousand were in prisons, homes for the aged, and other institutions.

Six hundred thousand were residents of the District of Columbia, a never-never land of Americans who count as taxpayers but not as voters.

Three hundred thousand were members of the armed forces who could not qualify for absentee ballots.

This leaves a total of 15.5 million Americans who simply found it inconvenient—a good deal less inconvenient than it was for a Delta Negro or a bedridden centenarian—to go to the polls, and that figure would doubtless rise to around 20 million if we were to account for the duplications in the list above. Even if we allow for such disabilities as religious scruples and flat tires and agoraphobia, we are left face to face with a staggering number of Americans who thought it quite unimportant to act the parts of responsible citizens of a great democracy. In the off year 1958 this 15–20 million jumped to 30–35 million. If I may toss out two more fascinating statistics, 3.5 million Americans who made a choice in the presidential election of 1956 did not make a choice in the congressional race in their district, while perhaps 2 million spoiled or did not mark their presidential ballots.

To repeat the questions: Who are these people, and why don't they vote? To both questions we can give only poorly informed answers, for this is an area of political behavior in which much remains to be learned and much never will be. We do know, in answer to the first question, that sex, age, education, income, and many other factors have a distinct influence on political motivation. Almost all studies of the demography of voting agree that persons in the *first* category of the following pairs are *less likely to vote* than persons in the second:

Women than men. (The gap has narrowed in recent years.) [42]

Young people than middle-aged people. (Lowering the voting age from 21 to 18 would serve only to lower the percentage of the turnout in elections.)

Country people than city people.

Grade-school graduates than high-school graduates.

High-school graduates than college graduates.

Unskilled workers than skilled workers.

Skilled workers than professional people.

Low-income people than middle-income people.

Middle-income people than high-income people.

Protestants than Catholics.

Democrats than Republicans.[43]

We know, too, that persons who do not vote in an election like that of 1952 are unlikely to vote in any election, which is another way of saying that millions of Americans, including many of the 22.5 million we excused from the 1956 election, are "out of it" completely, so far out that nothing but force could ever get them to the polls.

Why do we have such a shabby voting record in the United States? In any country that does not drive its citizenry to the polls, something like ten persons in a hundred will fail to vote out of shyness, cussedness, indifference, fear, principle, or total lack of motivation. But such persons, surely, are no more numerous in the United States than in Canada or Britain or Italy. What, then, are the special disabilities that frustrate broader participation even in states like New York or Massachusetts? I would put my finger on three reasons for our record. The first is the fact that our Constitution, laws, and electoral practices put an unusual number of technical difficulties in the path of the would-be voter.[44] Under our federal pattern of government the states are primarily responsible for setting the conditions of the suffrage, and few of them have done anything to make it easier for us to qualify and vote. If we, like many other countries, had a national voting list, permanent or easy registration, a short ballot, a national holiday on election day, and, to sweeten the appeal, a small tax exemption for those who cast their votes, we too might get an 85 per cent turnout (at least outside the South) every four years.

A second reason, of indeterminate but visible influence, is the two-party system. There is little doubt that many voters see nothing to choose between the Tweedledumism of the Democrats and Tweedledeeism of the Republicans. Lacking any third choice, they fail to choose at all. An interesting variation on the accepted pattern of nonvoting behavior was recorded by Lubell and others in the 1952 elections. There seem to have been a sizable number of Americans whom indecision rather than indifference or cynicism kept from the polls. Many nonvoters were anything but apathetic. They followed the campaign closely, indeed much too closely, for they apparently ended up paralyzed by the desire to vote for both candidates. They abstained from voting, not because they disliked Eisenhower and Stevenson, but rather because they liked them both so much that they could not make a choice that would leave one of them out in the cold. Thereby they proved a point that students of political behavior had known for some years: that "cross-pressures" can force many would-be participants in the political process to withdraw for a time, or even for good, into a state of indifference.[45]

Finally, we must take note of the paradoxical fact that the weakness of our electoral performance is a strange sign of the strength of our democracy. A free man goes to the polls because he is motivated to do so, and surely some part of his motivation arises out of the assumption that the results of the election will make a difference in his life. The plain fact is that, quite apart from the dampening effects of two-party politics, the results of elections make less of a difference in the lives of Americans than they do, let us say, in the lives of Frenchmen or Italians or South Africans. For this reason if for no other, political motivation is relatively low in America. Since we expect less from politics, we give less to it. Since we have confidence that the next election will take place on schedule, we find it harder to get excited about the current election—and so, of course, do our friends in Britain and Canada.[46] When ballots become bullets, Americans will be found casting them (or firing them) as willingly as any other people.

A final ingredient of the peculiar spirit of American politics is the strong antipolitical bias that crops up in our folklore. Parties as institutions and politicians as people both rank low in our scale of values. Politics is sin, and politicians, if not sinners, are pretty suspicious fellows. Every study of the 1952 election shows that Eisenhower picked up a decisive bundle of votes among people (many of them, incidentally, chronic nonvoters) who rejoiced in a candidate said to be "clean of politics" or "above politics" or "not a politician at all." In a country in which parties have played an essential role for more than 150 years, many of us have not moved one inch beyond the fears and prejudices of the Farewell Address in which Washington warned us solemnly against "the baneful effects of the spirit of party." In a country in which politicians have been the brokers of democracy, many of us would rather have our sons be anything—even "bookies" or jingle writers—than professional Democrats or Republicans. Again despite the efforts of civics teachers and ex-Presidents and public-spirited men of Madison Avenue, we are unwilling to look upon politics as a profession even remotely as attractive and important as medicine or law or teaching (or advertising). Lacking respect for politics as a calling, we assume that its ethical standards are bound to be depressed. Honesty in business is one thing, and revelations of corruption come as a shock. Honesty in politics is another, and revelations of corruption make us yawn. Old Simon Cameron, we would agree, had the truth by the tail when he defined an "honest politician" as "a man who, when he's bought, stays bought."

Like any observer of the political scene, I feel a strong temptation to moralize over the fact that most Americans are side-liners or even absentees in the great game of politics. For the time being I am going to resist the temptation and confine myself to the single observation that both our moralizings about nonparticipation and our attempts to stimulate interest would make more sense if they were based on the realities of American democracy. This is one dark area in which we could use a lot more light. We need more leads like David Riesman's precocious insight about the "new-style indifferents":

This apathy of the great majority is not the classic, quiescent indifference of the tradition-directed. It is to a large degree the indifference of people who know enough about politics to reject it, enough about political information to refuse it, enough about their political responsibilities as citizens to evade them.[47]

We need more careful studies like that of Woodward and Roper, which produced Table 1.

Table 1. Amount of Political Activity Exhibited by Various
Subgroups in the Population [48]

	Percentage within each subgroup who are politically			
	Very active	Fairly active	Fairly inactive	Very inactive
Subgroups				
"A" economic level (4% of total)	36	33	23	8
Executives	34	29	28	9
Professional people	31	32	25	12
Stockholders	28	30	30	12
College-educated	24	28	30	18
"B" economic level (10%)	24	26	34	16
Republicans	15	21	39	25
Men	13	19	36	32
People 50 years of age and over	12	17	34	37
People 35–49 years	11	19	39	31
"C" economic level (52%)	11	19	38	32
White people	11	17	36	36
Farmers	11	14	35	40
Independents in politics	10	21	37	32
Total adult population	10	17	35	38
People with only high-school education	9	17	40	34
Democrats	9	15	37	39
Nonstockholders	8	15	37	40
Women	8	14	33	45
People 21–34 years of age	8	14	32	46
Laboring people	6	14	37	43
Housewives	6	14	34	46
People with only grade-school education	5	11	33	51
Negroes	5	10	25	60
"D" economic level (34%)	3	9	31	57

Above all, we need the air cleared of cant and slogan making about this whole question of participation in politics. To listen to the well-intentioned but ill-informed pleas of the "Get-out-the-Vote-ers," one would think that the preservation of American democracy was a simple matter of increasing political enthusiasm. Would that it were!

These, then, appear to be the major characteristics of the American political system: (1) the persistence and ascendancy of the two-party scheme, (2) the hard times of minor parties devoted to narrow-gauge interests or broad-scale reform, (3) the loose, supple, interest-directed, principle-shunning, coalition-forming nature of the two major parties, (4) the decentralization of authority in the organization of these parties in the country at large, (5) the absence of effective discipline in the organization of these parties within the government, (6) the encirclement and penetration of the parties by a vigorous array of interest groups, and (7) the generally low-key, independent, skeptical approach of most Americans to the business of politics. There are other characteristics one could mention—venerability, moderation, pragmatism, conservatism—but they will emerge in due course in the chapters to come. Enough has been said already to make the main point with conviction. Nowhere in the world, not even in the nightmares of our friendly critics from abroad, is there a pattern of politics anything like ours.

II

The Functions of American Parties

PARTIES, it could be argued, exist primarily to serve the interests of the men who lead or support them. They are justified by their fruits, by which I mean the fruits that are showered on the leaders in the form of power and on the supporters in the form of favors. This, however, is a crude and narrow view of the role of parties in our society; for whatever they may have been in their beginnings, parties are now public institutions rather than private preserves. They stand closer to Congress and the courts than they do, say, to the American Legion or General Motors or the A.F.L.-C.I.O. on the spectrum of social organization that runs from the very private to the totally official. They are justified by their functions, by which I mean functions that are performed as services to the entire nation. We tolerate and even celebrate their existence because they do things for us in the public realm that would otherwise be done poorly or not at all.

Let us turn now to look at our parties in this light. Let us describe the political and social functions of any party in any democracy, and see how well our particular parties have performed each of these functions in our peculiar democracy.

Let us see, too, if there are any special, "characteristically American" functions that they have been called upon to perform or, more accurately, have performed without knowing it. Then perhaps we will be in a position to pass meaningful judgment on the quality of service rendered by the American party system to the American people.

The primary function of a political party in a democracy such as ours is to control and direct the struggle for power. From this function all others derive naturally.[1] I trust that no apologies need be made for calling attention to the fact that the political process in a free country is essentially a conflict, limited and regularized but nonetheless relentless, among groups of men who have contradictory interests and more or less mutually exclusive hopes of securing them. In the coming day of the golden utopia of communism, so Marx and Khrushchev have both promised us, there will be enough of everything to go all the way around—from crepes suzettes to psychological security by way of shoes and vitamins and love. Until that day, however, we will all be living in societies where there is a scarcity of the things that can be won by collective action, where, for instance, rich men cannot have low taxes and poor men free medical care at the same time. The struggle for political power, and for the privileges and immunities that political power can be made to produce, will go forward without rest, even in Khrushchev's coming society.

It is one of the aspirations of democracy to bring this struggle as much as possible into the open. It is the great purpose of political parties, the handmaidens of democracy, to bring the struggle under control: to institutionalize it with organization, to channel it through nominations and elections, to publicize it by means of platforms and appeals, above all to stabilize it in the form of that traditional quadrille in which the Ins and the Outs change places from time to time on a signal from the voters. The parties did not create the struggle for power; it would go on merrily without them. It would go on, however, much less purposefully and effectively and openly, and we might well be more grateful to our own parties for their modest efforts to bring under benevolent control the eternal conflict of interests described by Madison in *The Federalist*, no. 10. Just how grateful we should be is a question I will try to answer at the end of this review of the functions of parties.

The first of what we might call the subsidiary functions of a party in a democracy (subsidiary, that is, to the great, inclusive function we have just noted) is to act as an immense personnel agency. Constitutions make frugal provision for the election or appointment of persons to high office, but they extend no aid at all to those persons in and out of government who must act as recruiters. Statutes and ordinances bloom in profusion to create the rules and rewards of a civil service, but they offer no guaranty that the men on top of the permanent bureaucracy will be like-minded enough to give it a sense of cohesion or alert enough to the needs of the public to give it a sense of direction.

This is exactly where parties enter the picture decisively and why, all things considered, we could hardly do without them.[2] Willingly and indeed eagerly they set up and operate the machinery that places men and women in public office, and they do it at four key points: *nominations*, for they are organized to do the preliminary sifting of aspirants to elective office or, if necessary, to go out and recruit them actively; *campaigns*, for they make known to the voting public the credentials and promises of the narrowed list of candidates; *elections*, for they can provide (in bulk and at small cost) the swarm of citizens needed to man the polls and count the votes; and *appointments*, for they are no less eager to assist in the selective process than they are in the elective process. Indeed, they can come up even more quickly with a reasonably qualified candidate for appointment as Secretary of State or district attorney or recorder of deeds than with an equally qualified candidate for election as President or assemblyman or county coroner.

There are, of course, other techniques for recruiting men and women into the service of the community. The machinery of election is vigorously nonpartisan in two states and many cities in the United States, and the machinery appears to work fairly well. In the case of nominations for local office a caucus of all interested citizens is often the most sensible method of narrowing the field. And it is hard to deny that we could push the line dividing partisan from career appointments in, let us say, the diplomatic service well up the ladder with no injury to efficiency or team-mindedness. Yet this is the way we have chosen to do this important job, and there is much to be said for the choice of agents we have made—the major parties. They bring order out of disorder, simplicity out of diversity, precision out of chaos. They comb the population for willing and (more often than legend would have it) able recruits; and, by placing their tags upon these aspirants for election or appointment, they help us all, even in a country where tags can sometimes be misleading, to make more rational choices.

How would we ever get through the process of electing a Congress if the parties did not take over the primaries and elections? How would the President ever find candidates for several thousand offices a year if his party's informal patronage machinery were not quick with suggestions? How would we go about filling the 750,000 (give or take 100,000) elective offices in the United States if we were a strictly nonpartisan people? If we do not get as many first-rate men as we should in Congress and the administration, in state legislatures and school boards, the blame must be laid at the doors of the people with their antipolitical mores and not of the politicians with their vulgar methods. The latter, after all, stay in business by pleasing the former, and up to now they seem to have pleased us well enough. This, in any case, is the wonderfully symbiotic relationship that we, like all other democracies, have created. The process of nomination and election needs parties to make it go; parties make nominations and fight elections or they are not parties at all. Small wonder that the parties have been given legal status throughout the United States and that the state legislatures have chosen increasingly to regulate their structure and operation in considerable detail.[3]

Parties can also serve as important sources of public policy. They have no monopoly of this function, to be sure, nor should they in the kind of pluralistic society we identify with democracy. The great and small policies by which we live emerged first as special pleadings of an infinite variety of groups and persons, and we should be happy to live in a society in which organizations like N.A.M. or N.A.A.C.P. and men like Walter Lippmann or Bernard Baruch come up constantly with new proposals for our consideration. Yet the parties—and in this instance I include third parties—are perhaps best fitted of all agencies to convert formless hopes or frustrations into proposals that can be understood, debated, and, if found appealing, approved by the people. Because they are the only truly national, multi-interest, broadly based organizations active in our society (the only ones, indeed, that we can permit to be active), they are uniquely situated to originate policies themselves or to broaden the special pleadings of other men and groups. Their policies, moreover, are likely to be a little more realistic than those that emerge from the paid researches of interest groups, for any one policy must be fitted with dozens of others into a full program for governing the nation.

Thanks to the fuzzy nature of our political system, the major parties have not been especially effective in performing this function. In the words of the Committee on Political

Parties of the American Political Science Association, "the American two-party system has shown little propensity for evolving original or creative ideas about public policy; it has even been rather sluggish in responding to such ideas in the public interest." [4] The platforms of the parties, which are presumably the most eloquent statements they can make of their current intentions, have never been noted for originality or clarity. One cannot fail to be impressed by some of the reports of the Democratic Advisory Council or by the Report of the Republican Committee on Program and Progress, *Decisions for a Better America*, issued in September 1959, yet one is struck by the scarcity of concrete proposals in all these reports and bound to wonder if the members of these committees really speak with the voice of authority. Yet the remembrance of Wilson's New Freedom and Roosevelt's New Deal should be enough to convince us that parties can originate policies, and that their policies, unlike those of most interest groups, can cut a broad swath through American life. Wilson and especially Roosevelt took their policies wherever they found them, but some of the most important were first given form by lieutenants acting consciously as Democrats.

The point at which our parties may indeed have failed us in this matter of policies is not in originating or formulating or advertising them, but in converting them into the hard coin of purposeful law and skillful administration. Before we can go into that problem, however, we must take note of the function that makes it possible and even mandatory for parties in a democracy to put their policies into effect: the organization and operation of government. Within every true party there exists, as I pointed out in Chapter I, a governmental party, a hard core of officeholders whose duty to the community goes beyond mere electioneering or even formulating policies. If this party has been victorious in the most recent election, it is expected to organize the legislative and executive branches and to run them with the aid of the appeals and disciplines of party loyalty. In the United States, of course, the ground rules of the Constitution make it necessary for a party to win several elections over a period of time in order to exercise the kind of over-all control that comes in one large bundle to the majority party (or coalition) under the rules of the parliamentary system, but in all democratic countries the principle is the same: every self-respecting party is, in effect, a miniature state that must be prepared to take over and operate the real state (or some portion of it) at the command of the electorate. A political organization unwilling to govern is not, by any definition, a party.

To cite the example closest to home, in 1956 we asked Mr. Eisenhower, in his capacity as victorious candidate for the Presidency under the aegis of the Republican party, to wield his own powers and to supervise the execution of the laws of the United States with the aid of a large team of men drawn almost exclusively from the ranks of his party. He and his colleagues promised us to operate the executive branch in a certain way and for certain purposes, and we, in effect, turned the levers of public power over to them. They also promised to account to us as a party in the next election for the way in which they had manipulated these levers—or so at least runs the theory of party responsibility in a democracy.

At the same time, and in a unique demonstration of political cussedness, we asked Mr. Rayburn and Senator Johnson, in their capacities as leaders of the victorious party in the congressional elections, to organize the two houses of our national legislature and run them with the help of all kinds of party machinery—floor leaders, whips, committee chairmen, policy committees, and the rest.[5] This they were expected to do, as men have done for generations, with as much conviction and precision as one can ever get out of the American party system, and they, too, promised to be held accountable as a party. So it goes all down through the kaleidoscopic structure of government in the United States. Although we try to remove parts of it—a board here, a city there—from the arena of the party struggle, we rely overwhelmingly on our political parties to organize and operate the agencies of the public will. For example, in almost every state legislature where two-party politics exists at all, the majority party exercises tight control over formal organization and procedures.[6] This is one of those things which, as some people like to say, is "done better in England," where constitutional government takes on the form, openly and proudly, of party government. Yet even in America we would be at a loss how to get on with the public business if the parties were not always around begging us to lease them the concession.

If we have few complaints about the technical competence with which our majority parties organize and operate the agencies of government, we have many, probably more than any other people in the democratic world, about the skill and dedication they bring to the process of making their own policies the policies of city or state or nation; and that, as I have already indicated, is one of the basic functions of a party in a democracy: to make concrete promises to the electorate and then, if invited by the electorate to govern, to make good on those promises. There are promises and promises, to be sure, and the imperatives of democracy demand that a major shift in public policy be carried through only by a clear majority in answer to a clear invitation. Yet if this function is not the essence of party government, what is? If parties will not take the lead in making policy for the community, what groups will? In the ideal democracy, it could be argued, responsible parties would exercise command, if never enjoy a monopoly, of the process of decision making. We would always know whom to punish for unkept promises and wrong guesses.

No country comes close to being an ideal democracy, and, in this instance at least, America does not come close at all. American parties are notoriously delinquent in keeping their promises to the electorate. We have become especially skeptical about the capacity of the majority party in Congress, no matter how smashing its most recent electoral triumph, to build new structures of law and administration out of the planks in its platform. To tell the truth, most of us do not find this skepticism hard to bear, and the complaints are voiced more in sorrow than in anger. The fact is that we have never been as willing as the British or Swedes or Belgians or even the Canadians to consign to partisan hands the great process of decision making for the nation. We seem to be happier with decisions that have been adopted on a bipartisan or, even better, nonpartisan basis, more willing to live with laws that have been approved finally by a majority of both parties in Congress—and for which neither party can properly take primary credit. Yet in adopting this easygoing attitude, we are hacking at the roots of responsible party government. If parties are not expected or encouraged to make good on their reasonable promises, then other groups less open in operation and accountable in fact—blocs and interest groups and loose coalitions of lobby-ridden legislators—will assume the authority to make public policy.

The last of what we might call the political functions of parties in a democracy is one that a party does not choose happily yet must accept willingly if the burden is thrust upon it. This is the delicate function, so necessary to democracy and so incomprehensible to autocracy, of "loyal opposition." It is, of course, the special province of the party that has lost the last election. The minority party is expected to organize itself in the legislature for the primary purpose of checking the majority party. Members of the party are not rigidly forbidden to be creative statesmen, and in any session many occasions will arise when they will join with the majority, as individuals or even as a party, in enacting measures that cut across partisan lines or do not appear as partisan at all. For the most part, however, their task is essentially negative in character and purpose. They must oppose the proposals of the majority, develop alternative proposals for the electorate to consider at the next election, and keep a close watch on those who are executing the laws under the direction of the majority party. Like any other task we assign to our parties, this function admits of abuse. Few politicians in the ranks of the minority pay careful attention to the rough line between responsible opposition and irresponsible pugnacity. Yet it is a function that we could ill do without, for so long as the majority party is expected to govern, so long must the minority party be encouraged to oppose.

American parties have had perhaps more success in opposing than in governing, which is a revealing commentary on the nature of our political system. In fact, it often seems that American politicians are happier out of power than in it. Like the great Constitution under which we live serenely, our political instinct seems to prefer restraint to power and delay to action. The minority, finding its role more congenial than does the majority, performs it with a relish that is usually missing in the activities of the governing party. The framers of the Constitution were concerned, on one hand, to construct a system of checks and balances and, on the other, to make it difficult for parties to arise and prosper. Would they be shocked or merely surprised to learn that one of the most effective checks in our enduring system of checks and balances is the party in opposition, and that it is, moreover, the kind of check these loyal Newtonians liked best of all—fluid, kinetic, and, in the words of John Adams, opposing "power to power, force to force, strength to strength, interest to interest, as well as reason to reason, eloquence to eloquence, passion to passion"?

To this list of the political functions of parties in a democracy we can add three others that might more accurately be described as social, since in performing them parties serve men in their roles as social rather than political animals. First, parties are important agencies in the educational process. The citizens of a free country must be instructed in the practices of democracy and kept informed on the issues of their times, not merely to become more forceful agents of public opinion and more skillful voters, but also to live more satisfying lives. Once they have finished the last stage of their formal education, they must rely on a battery of informal instruments ranging from Sunday afternoon television to word of mouth. Political parties are at best crude instruments of adult education, yet they can do much to compel study and discussion of important problems.

American parties have given over perhaps too much of their own responsibility for adult education to interest groups, yet our history is full of instances in which a party took the lead in educating the public to recognize and understand the facts of a new condition or trend in American life. The Republican party, speaking through men like Lincoln, did much to educate the nation in the true nature and implications of slavery. The Democratic party, speaking through Franklin Roosevelt and his friends, did even more to educate us in the proper relations of private enterprise and public authority. Third parties, too, although their student bodies have been limited, have scored real successes as educating agencies. The parties could certainly afford to do a great deal more in performing this function, especially in stimulating interest in politics. The "seminars" and "schools" now being run every year in several parts of the country could be multiplied many times over to the benefit of American minds and American democracy. Even these present modest efforts are welcome additions to the vast, jerry-built structure of adult education. The citizen who goes to school cautiously with our political parties can get an excellent education in subjects that really count.

Next, the parties serve a useful social purpose in acting as buffers and adjusters between individuals and society, especially as the latter intrudes into the lives of ordinary persons in the shape of impersonal political authority.[7] The days are pretty well over when big and little bosses did much (for a consideration, to be sure) to soften the impact of the city on the sensibilities of helpless and ignorant people—when Nocky Johnson of Atlantic City kept a pile of coal to which any poor Negro could come for a free bagful; when George Washington Plunkitt handed out jobs along with free advice; when Frank Skeffington (or was it James Curley, or Spencer Tracy?) acted the part of the bountiful city squire; when Walter Lippmann doubted that the City of New York could ever be "as human, as kindly, as jolly as Tammany Hall"; [8] and when Martin Lomasney of Boston spoke for all the old machines: "I think that there's got to be in every ward somebody that any bloke can come to—no matter what he's done—and get help. Help, none of your law and justice, but help." [9]

Yet the parties are still important dispensers of those aids, favors, and immunities (for example, from prosecution of father for peddling without a license or son for breaking windows) that make it possible for men and women to live reasonably confident lives in a harsh environment. If poor Negroes in Atlantic City no longer need to be given coal, they do need help in obtaining unemployment compensation with which to buy coal. The more penetrating and complicated the power of government becomes, the more demand there is for skilled "adjusters," who might as well be politicians as priests or social workers. There is, of course, a seamy side to this function; politicians contribute more than their fair share to the corruptions and injustices of American life, in the country as well as in the city. Yet the fact that a function is performed corruptly is no decisive argument against its being performed in the first place. Men need buffers against both state and society, and they must take them as and where they find them. In the local organizations of political parties Americans have found buffers of uncommon efficiency. The lives of millions of Americans would have been much harder to bear if the parties had not done their work as agencies of social welfare.

Finally, parties serve a symbolic function—or should we start from the other direction and call it psychological?—by providing an object, large and friendly and often exciting, to which men can extend allegiance. Graham Wallas, in his memorable study of *Human Nature in Politics*, was perhaps the first observer to isolate and examine this function. Having taken note of the multitude of voters and of the psychical inability of any one voter to deal with more than a few men and ideas, he went on: "Something is required simpler and more permanent, something which can be loved and trusted, and which can be recognized at successive elections as being the same thing that was loved and trusted before; and a party is such a thing." [10]

I have said already that parties in America are not churches. Let me amend that observation by suggesting that for many Americans the party is like a church, but on the Unitarian rather than the Catholic model, that is, a church that makes few demands and exercises no discipline. In the words of Professors Merriam and Gosnell:

The party is more human than the state, more approachable, more intimate in its relations than the government. . . . The party is in a sense a political church which does not require very regular attendance or have a very strict creed; but still it provides a home and it "looks after" the individual if he pays the minimum of party *devoirs*. . . . Or, changing the metaphor, the party is a sporting interest, like a baseball team in which the individual is intensely interested from time to time. [11]

American parties have played this important role rather more diffidently and sloppily than they have most of their other roles, but in so doing they have been, as always, "characteristically American." I have a feeling that, if our politicians were to get the kind of allegiance they are often heard to claim, they would not know what to do with it.

In the effectiveness with which they perform most of these political and social functions, parties in America fall well short of the ideal of democracy or even of the reality of parties in many other countries. They are especially ineffectual in the task of formulating policies and transforming them into governmental programs, and thus they get only low marks for their performance of the great, overriding function of channeling and disciplining the struggle for power. No matter how indulgently we judge them, we are bound to conclude that parties are not nearly as important factors in the decision-making process in America as they are in most other democracies. Blocs, interest groups, bipartisan coalitions, and nonpartisan elites all challenge the parties constantly for control of the key stages in the political process.

An American party is a relatively weak agent of decision and power primarily because it is the kind of party I described in Chapter I—broad in appeal, moderate in outlook, loose-jointed in structure, tolerant in discipline, uncommitted in ideology, one of two parties in a political system that plays down principle and plays up accommodation. It is that kind of party for dozens of reasons that are spread all along the course of American history. I cannot linger to give a full accounting of these reasons, but I can suggest the main areas into which we would have to go exploring for them.

We would have to look first at the Constitution, which has had (and must continue to have) a far more powerful influence on the style of our politics and shape of our parties than many political scientists oriented to psychology and sociology would have us believe. Almost every command, prohibition, or arrangement in this document has helped to dictate the direction in which our parties have developed. The division of power and even of sovereignty between nation and states is a major cause of decentralization in the parties. This fact of federalism, strengthened by the physical separation of the legislature and the executive, makes a mockery of all hopes for strong party discipline. The method of electing congressmen and, even more obviously, the President dooms the first two parties to lives of incessant compromise and all other parties to frustration. The Presidency itself, at once the most political and least political of offices, cuts across the neat lines of party responsibility. And the whole spirit of the Constitution, a document that remains even today a catalogue of limitations, insists so strongly that many decisions of a public character be taken by private persons and agencies that it is no wonder our parties are encouraged to be all things to all men in many areas of controversy.

Behind the Constitution stand the American people, and surely we would have to look next at their assumptions, myths, and prejudices for an explanation of the peculiar quality of American parties. I realize that I am skating on thin ice; I am highly suspicious myself of writers who attribute an attitude or trait to an entire people. Still, there are generalizations that are demonstrably truer of the minds of a random sample of Americans than those of a similar sample of Britons or Austrians or Peruvians, and some of these generalizations are full of implications for our parties. We are said to be a people with a prejudice against politics, and that may explain why our parties tolerate so many mavericks, men who claim to be "Americans first and party men second," even in the front ranks. We are said to be a people with a pragmatic cast of mind, and that may explain why we permit the parties to pursue their seemingly absurd ways, asking only that the results make sense. Above all we are said to be a people with scant respect for fine points of doctrine, and that goes far to explain the weakness of ideological commitment in our successful parties.

There are plenty of ideological Americans, and the num-

ber may be growing, but they are still far from numerous or
ideological enough to force our parties to take stronger
stands on doctrinal issues. A people's institutions must reflect
the broad features of their character. If American parties have
small use for sharply honed ideology, that is because so many
Americans have even less. While the parties are by now both
cause and effect of our refusal to engage in sharp distinctions
of doctrine, the main influence has been visited by the people on the parties. If ideology does play a part in shaping the
parties, it does it in a rough and offhanded way by forcing
them to stand for many of the same principles. If we think
only a few large thoughts about the nature of society and the
purpose of government, we think them strongly—and we
think them in common. The American consensus is unique
in its virility and broad appeal. Our interests, which are many,
are remarkably diverse; our principles, which are few, are
remarkably uniform. The natural product of this powerful national consensus is a pair of parties that overlap substantially in
their attempts to prove their loyalty to it.

The last place in which we would look for an explanation
of the peculiar nature of American parties, and thus of their
undistinguished performance in the struggle for power, would
be the history of the parties themselves. It is a fact of small
repute but great moment—I would hail it as the paramount
fact in this whole book—that our parties have had thrust
upon them functions other and perhaps more important than
those that are considered the natural functions of a party in a
democracy. They have performed these without conscious
purpose and for their own selfish ends; they have rarely laid
claim to the glory that is their due for performing them so
well. Yet if they had not done them, we would be a far different and, in my opinion, unhappier country, and they
would be far different and, in the opinion of some writers,
happier parties. The point for us to keep in mind is that their
willingness to take on these historic functions has had a pro-

found impact on their structures, principles, and methods. In order to serve the American people in the capacities I am about to describe, the parties have had to eschew discipline, suppress doctrine, and fragment power.

To put the matter as simply as possible, they are the parties they are today because they have played a vital role in creating the unity of America. They are weak agents in the struggle for power because they have been strong agents in the course of our rise to nationhood. It has been their historic mission to hold the line against some of the most powerful centrifugal forces in American society, and their success in performing it can be measured with considerable accuracy in their peculiar habits. No one should pass judgment on American parties until he understands that fact and has reviewed the whole record of their achievements. Let us now move on with our own review by taking careful note of the contributions our major parties have made to national unity in checking the forces of disunity.

The first of these forces is sectionalism, which lies so deep in the American way of life and has exerted such an attraction on American minds and passions that the wonder is we are one country at all and not a parcel of squabbling Balkan states. We were by no means destined to become one nation extending its claims to allegiance over all the land between Canada and Mexico and between the two great oceans. The Union got off to a shaky start; it was challenged boldly in the nineteenth century by every section of the country in turn; several sections seem to have been at perpetual odds with it. One section, indeed, as we will never be allowed to forget, made an agonizing attempt to break loose completely, and only the force of arms kept the eleven Southern states in the Union—or, as some prefer, brought them back into it.

What had kept them in the Union up to the break of 1861 and was to bring them back after 1865 was the force of politics, which has always been—next to a common language, common needs, and common memories—the most powerful centripetal force in American society. The parties, especially the Whigs before the Civil War and the Democrats both before and after, have acted as skillful brokers of sectional interests. In their efforts to build up a majority in the country, they have reached out into all sections for support, have drawn on all sections for officeholders and voters, and have tried to make the special interests of each section the interests of the whole nation. Always adept at bargaining and compromise, the parties have gone far to build up an acceptable consensus among the elites in every part of the land. Needless to say, they have not always found this task easy. The Republicans, in particular, have had their troubles being a national party; even today there lingers upon them that scent of Northern and Western sectionalism that in 1856 alerted the sensitive nostrils of the South to the realization that the old rules no longer held and that the Union might be about to disintegrate.

The force of politics as a nationalizing influence demonstrated its historic importance most dramatically in its one hour of failure. The collapse of the Whigs, for all their unattractiveness the most truly national party in American history, and the swift emergence of the Republicans, the most unhappily sectional of all major parties, put thinking Americans on the alert. The failure of the Democrats to nominate Stephen A. Douglas at Charleston in the spring of 1860, the withdrawal of the slave-state delegations to Richmond and the Douglas men to Baltimore, and the consequent victory of the Republicans under Lincoln were a series of hammer blows that sent the Union sprawling.[12] The fact for us to remember is that the last institution to break apart in the crisis of slavery and sectionalism was a political party—not a church or lodge or interest group—and the first to be reunited after the resolution of the crisis by force of arms was the same political party. By stretching out their hands for the votes of their old friends in the South in 1866 and 1868, the Democrats did more to restore the Union than did any other group or force in or out of power. To round out this revealing story of disunion and union, we might recall that the parties brought off the famous deal of 1877 that cemented the South politically in the Union. In return for an agreement by the Democrats not to challenge the shaky results of the election of 1876, the Republicans promised to withdraw federal troops from the South.[13] This was a classic demonstration of the whole process I have been describing. The motives were impure and the purposes selfish; the methods of decision were not those we write about so glibly in our tracts and texts on democracy. Yet there can be no doubt that the chief object of benefaction was the American Union. Men all through our history have proclaimed with fervor that there are things more important than the Union. In the full perspective of our history, however, I am not sure what they are.

Let me clinch this point with the help of one of the few non-American writers who seems to know what American politics is all about. Putting his finger eloquently on the great political lesson of the Civil War, Denis Brogan writes:

It can hardly be doubted that the immediate cause of the greatest breakdown of the American political system was the breakdown of the party system, the failure of the party machinery and the party leaders to remember their national function, which, if carried out, was the justification of the varied weakness and absurdities of the party organizations and policies. Not until the party system broke down, in the dissolution of the Whigs, in the schism of the Democrats, was war possible. . . .

Although it may be rash to suggest a belief in a national memory, it is at any rate possible that the American shrinking from doctrinaire parties, from people who knew their own minds, who would not compromise, who had a social theory to defend or attack, owed something to the recollection of the time when America *had* such parties, when, to the astonishment of each side, North and South found themselves at war.[14]

A second centrifugal force in American society against which the parties have held the line with success for us as well as for themselves—and with damage only to discipline and principle—is the divisive thrust of class and calling. Thanks to the happier social and economic climate of America, the free play of these closely related forces has never imperiled our unity half so dangerously as it has the unity of France, Italy, or even Britain. Yet the climate cannot be awarded all the credit for the limited impact on American unity of the eternal conflict of economic and social interests. The parties, too, have played their part in smothering the conflict. In the course of their unflagging search for the complicated formula of victory, they have appealed to all classes and interests as they have appealed to all sections, and almost every class and interest has wisely agreed that it is better to be a half-satisfied part of a rabble with some hope of victory than the dominant force in a disciplined army with no hope at all. Perhaps the class struggle in all its vigor and viciousness would never have come to tyrannize over America, yet there is no doubt that it has been kept even more safely at bay by the peculiar workings of our two-party system. So long as the Republicans bid powerfully for the votes of workingmen, so long as the Democrats can count on their share of businessmen and gentlemen, so long as both parties fall all over themselves wooing the increasingly perverse voters from the farms of America, this nation has less than other nations to fear from the always thinly veiled passions of social and economic division. Although our parties are perhaps more openly oriented to particular classes and economic interests than they were a generation ago, we are still far from a system in which the Haves and Have-Nots face each other suspiciously across a sharply drawn political line. When America finally spawns a genuine labor party, it will be a far different country from the one we have known, and I am fairly certain that the men of labor, in positions of command as well as in the ranks, will not like it any better than the rest of us.

The third force of disunity which the parties have done much to smother is the explosive power latent in the scrambled pattern of race, national origin, and religion. Almost every identifiable cultural group in American society has found a happier political home in one party than in the other. At least one major group in one part of the country, the Negroes in the South, has been fought off savagely by one of the parties, the Democrats. Still, the broad scheme of American politics has been one under which neither party could afford to write off any sizable group and under which most groups have divided evenly enough between the parties to create an illusion, and perhaps more than just an illusion, of unity amid diversity. Most of the particulars of this historic process are too well known to require extended comment: how millions of immigrants were given their first hearty welcome by a local boss; how the Democrats made good Americans out of Irishmen and the Republicans made equally good Americans out of Germans; how thousands of men shut off by a wall of prejudice from other paths to higher status made their way up the dizzy escalator of politics; how men of different tongues learned to speak the common language of politics; how Negroes in the North made progress in politics much faster than in any other area; how the parties tiptoed around the divisive issues of religion and thus gave them no chance to explode. Again one must confess that the picture is not all that pleasant. There is always something a little hard to swallow in the party ticket listing an upstate, old-stock Protestant for governor, a downstate Irish Catholic for lieutenant-governor, a suburban Jew for attorney-general, a large-city Italian for secretary of state, and a small-city Pole for comptroller, but if this kind of enterprise is one of the few to bring men of such diverse backgrounds together—and to invite each of their followings to cast a highly "tolerant" ballot—who can argue that the higher good of democratic unity has not been served, however casually and perversely?

In all these ways and in many more the parties have softened the rough edges of America's fabulous diversity. They have paid a stiff price in the coin of diminished reputation, for many articulate Americans continue to ask caustically, "Why don't they stand for anything different?"—indeed, "Why don't they stand for anything at all?" We have paid an even stiffer price in the coin of a nearly formless political process in which parties with too little power and interest groups with too much purpose struggle riotously over a darkling plain. Yet the feeling will not down that the price, although high, has not been exorbitant, and that what we have purchased with it—the unity of a free people—is more to be coveted than a politics that makes perfect sense. It would be helpful if more people realized that the peculiarities of our party system have been, in Herbert Agar's phrase, "the price of union," [15] but perhaps it is better for us to live in a system we only dimly comprehend.

This, in any case, is the essence of our political history: the parties have been the peacemakers of the American community, the unwitting but forceful suppressors of the "civil-war potential" we carry always in the bowels of our diverse nation.[16] Blessed are the peacemakers, I am tempted to conclude. They may never be called the children of God nor even inherit the earth, but they, after all, seek only to inherit the White House.

The parties have worked still other influences on American life, and we must take these into account before passing final judgment on their over-all performance. In the first place, for all their vulgarities and corruptions, they have contributed handsomely to the cause of American democracy. We are far from being the democracy we celebrate in song and slogan —that pearly string of "alabaster cities . . . undimmed by human tears"—but we are a long step nearer because of the mysterious operations of our parties. Surely we are more of a social democracy because the parties have gone to every group and class, however mean and despised, in search of votes. Millions of Americans received their first intimations of power and "belonging," indeed got their first generous helpings of liberty, equality, and fraternity, from the parties. And surely we are more of a political democracy because the parties pressed hard if not continuously for an expansion of the suffrage and of popular participation in the decision-making process. I repeat: Political parties and democracy are inseparable phenomena. The surge toward democracy first gave life to parties as we know them, and parties in their turn were major spurs to the onward course of democracy. It would, indeed, be hard to decide which was the chicken and which the egg here in America.

The democratizing influence of the parties has been visited with particular force on the Constitution. The Constitution did much to shape the parties, but they have given back almost as much as they have got. Schattschneider, in a brilliant metaphor, writes of the parties as "the river of American politics, the stream of the living impulse to govern," and of the Constitution as "the river bed, the firm land whose contour shapes the stream." The river is "the prisoner of the land" through which it flows, "but in the long run" it "can transform the landscape." [17]

Our parties have transformed the constitutional landscape primarily by broadening the base of American politics. For one thing, they have altered the whole system of electing the President. The nominating convention, the far-ranging campaign, the popular vote, the general-ticket system, the elimination of independent choice in the electoral college—all these and other party-inspired devices have converted the decentralized, nonpolitical, dignified system of election planned by the framers into the fabulous plebiscite that is today our leading national ritual and, all things considered, a remarkably effective procedure for choosing an able man to lead us. For another, the parties have democratized the selective as well as the elective process. Their impact on the President's constitutional power of appointment has been incalculable. Admittedly there was nothing polite about the spoils system— a party device if ever there was one—but its introduction in the early nineteenth century opened up the seats of power to men in all walks of life and made our government a far more popular affair. We let the parties push the use of this device much too far, to be sure, and the civil-service system is, in effect, a counterrevolution against the tyranny of politics. Even today, however, the system of patronage works to deepen the reservoir from which men and women are drawn for public service.

The parties have left their mark on the Constitution itself by taking an active part in the poky process through which we have added twelve amendments to the Constitution since the adoption of the Bill of Rights. The process of amendment demands a series of extraordinary majorities and thus cuts across party lines in search of both bipartisan and nonpartisan support. Yet it is hard to find a single amendment from number XII through number XXII that does not bear the imprint of one or both of our major parties or, deep below the surface, of some forgotten third party. To run through the list quickly:

Amendment XII, a useful addition, was inspired as much by the desire of the Jeffersonians to prevent the election of a Federalist Vice-President in 1804 as by a general unwillingness to go through another fiasco like the election of 1800.

Amendments XIII, XIV, and XV, the Civil War Amendments, were largely the work of the Radical Republicans in Congress. Ten of the eleven Southern states rejected the Fourteenth Amendment in 1866, thus postponing the restoration of their representation in Congress, and many Southern

Democrats have still not made peace with this "unconstitutional" part of the Constitution.

Amendments XVI (income tax), XVII (direct election of senators), XVIII (prohibition), and XIX (women's suffrage) were all products of years of agitation in which third parties, maverick wings of the major parties, and finally the leaders of one or both of the major parties played vital roles.

Amendment XX (the "lame duck" amendment) was a nonpartisan affair in which the leaders of the major parties—unable to look Senator George Norris in the eye—were willing to go along.

Amendment XXI (repeal of prohibition) was both a nonpartisan and bipartisan affair in which the Democratic platform of 1932 and Democratic candidates of 1928 and 1932 played catalytic parts.

Amendment XXII (forbidding third terms), a controversial addition indeed, was primarily a product of Republican partisanship.

The parties have also added their bit to the rise of the Presidency to a dominant if hardly dominating position in our scheme of government. By democratizing the procedure of election, they have helped to make it an essentially popular office. By inviting the President to serve as the grand sachem of the party that has elected him, they have given him new weapons of persuasion over the administration, Congress, and the people at large. And by confusing and delaying the process of policy making in Congress, they have unwittingly thrown upon him more authority to make policy himself than even a modernized system of the separation of powers would logically assign to him. The President, in a word, should be grateful to the parties.

So perhaps should all of us who are interested in making our Constitution an instrument of effective government. It has not been an easy constitution with which to make policy quickly and to govern efficiently, which is exactly the kind of constitution the framers intended it to be. The gaps that separate the executive from the legislature, the national government from the states, and the states from each other have often been as discouraging to men of good will as to men of corrupt intent. As we have often been told, this emphasis on restraint and delay was all very well in the eighteenth and even nineteenth centuries, but the twentieth century, the world of automation and atomic energy, is another kind of world, one in which we are as likely to be destroyed by a vacuum of power as by an overdose of it. For this reason we need more, and more easily traveled, bridges across these gaps, and our major parties provide two that we could hardly afford to be without. The simple fact that the President, roughly half of Congress, and roughly half of the state governors are all brothers in the same political lodge is one that certainly helps to close the gaps as well as to bridge them. If the parties continue to do their political, social, and historic tasks with even modest effectiveness, we need have few qualms about moving into the future with our pluralized form of government. They helped mightily to build the consensus that makes such government possible at all. They continue, in their own fantastic way, to keep the consensus alive and also to keep all our independent centers of power in touch with one another. For this, and for their willingness to organize and run our countless units of government, we might well render them more thanks than they usually get.

We can render them thanks for many more reasons than that and, in the same breath, take polite issue with the Washington of the Farewell Address, who for once was wrong in insisting that "the spirit of party" was the "worst enemy" of popular government. Admittedly this is the sort of judgment that the historian makes in his role as impressionist rather than scientist, but it is hard to think of any major American institution—corporation, union, church, college, public school, family, or any agency of government except perhaps the

Presidency itself—that has performed its many functions any more effectively and benevolently than has the political party. We could even say that its one acknowledged failure has not been, in the larger sense, a failure at all. If the parties have been weak agents in the struggle for power, contractors unable to deliver on many of their most solemn promises to the electorate, this has been because a majority of the electorate has rarely been clear-eyed and clear-cut enough to know and get what it wants. When such a majority exists, it gets what it wants, even in our obstructive system; but such a majority emerges only rarely in the circumstances of American life. For all our self-congratulatory talk of innovation and progress, we are politically a most conservative people, and we have relied heavily, if somewhat shamefacedly, on our parties to slow down the pace of progress.

In this light the American two-party system appears as one of the truly conservative arrangements in the world of politics, a system designed by accident or providence to delay, check, and frustrate the ill-digested plans of men while permitting them to govern in a responsible and popular manner. The two-party system works to lengthen the delays built into the constitutional process. It is not the stubborn presence of the minority party but the opportunistic give-and-take of both parties that is the great auxiliary check and balance in the American pattern of free government. It was not to use political power imaginatively and purposefully in order to remake society that we called our parties into being, but to render the mechanics of government more comprehensible and efficient. It was not the use but the abuse of power with which we were first of all concerned, and we agreed almost instinctively to adopt a political system that would make both more difficult.

Up to now, at least, we have had little reason to complain of the pattern of political compromise worked out by history to serve our peculiar ends. If the struggle for power has not been disciplined, it has also not been exacerbated. If our parties have not governed enough, they have also not governed too much. They have helped to build a nation out of the scourings of a half-hundred nations, a union out of the scuffle of sectional and local urges. They have helped to make a difficult Constitution work far more smoothly than its framers had any right to expect. Over the long span of American history they have done few things we did not want them to do, and done most things we wanted them to do. Like the public schools of America, the parties must be judged finally as institutions called upon by history to go far beyond their precise mission. The schools have had to do more than educate; the parties have had to do more than govern.

The more one contemplates our political history, the more certain it seems that *these* parties were designed prescriptively to serve the purposes of *this* people under the terms of *this* Constitution. They are the natural fruits of a unique way of life. The politics they play is thus a unique politics. It is not the politics of democracy in the abstract or of British democracy—with which it is always being compared unfavorably—but of American democracy, a way of life with unique needs and problems. In this light alone can it be understood and assessed.

III

Democrats and Republicans:
Who Are They?

THE party struggle has been kicking up the dust on the American scene for more than a century and a half. It was brought to life by the clash of interests in the first years under the Constitution, took form in the elections of 1796, 1798, and 1800, and, except for that unique pause for breath known as the Era of Good Feelings, has been pursued without rest down to this day—whence it will be pursued without further rest so long as this country is governed on principles of constitutional democracy.

Some historians, following the lead of John Adams, place the emergence of parties much farther back in the course of American history. "You say 'our divisions began with federalism and anti-federalism,'" Adams wrote to William Keteltas in 1812. "Alas! they began with human nature; they have existed in America from its first plantation. In every colony, divisions always prevailed. In New York, Pennsylvania, Virginia, Massachusetts, and all the rest, a court and country party have always contended." [1] Rather than trace the development of American politics back to the Ins and Outs at Jamestown in 1619 or even, as Adams would have preferred, to Adam and the Serpent in the Garden of Eden, let us fix on the decade before the election of 1800 as the gestatory period of American parties. This famous election (over which Adams had a right to cry "alas!") was fought by two opposing groups of like-minded public and private men which we can recognize, even from this distance, as political parties.

Even this modest claim is enough to put us first among all nations in the development of parties as agencies of constitutional government. The British must be credited with the invention of parties *in* government, but we were the first in the field with extragovernmental organizations to support the intragovernmental divisions.[2] The American party system is the oldest in the world, and for this reason, if for no other, we might well be prouder of it, especially because priority in the development of parties is dramatic testimony of priority in the development of constitutional democracy. We have noted this point before, and we will note it again before this book is finished: Parties and democracy arose together; they have lived and prospered in a closely symbiotic relationship; and if one of them should ever weaken and die, the other would die with it. The condition of a nation's parties is trustworthy evidence of the health of its democratic values and institutions. One must, of course, be careful in reading the evidence. In matters like morality and morale there may be a one-to-one correlation between the vigor of a democracy and the condition of its parties, whereas in matters like organizational strength and commitment to principle the correlation may be a great deal more subtle. In any case he who knows all there is to know about the political parties in a democracy knows much of what he needs to know about the state of its values and institutions.

Let me try to make my own small contribution to a better understanding of the present state and future prospects of

American democracy by examining our political parties with a critical eye. When I say "political parties" I do not mean a series of abstract agglomerates floating about in the heavenly city of political theory. I mean a pair of real parties, visible entities with legal status, organization, records, and bank accounts, that have dominated our political landscape since 1856 and have now moved beyond mere domination to a point where they may be said to "hog" it. I mean the Democratic party and the Republican party, each of which I propose to examine in the course of the next three chapters in terms of (1) current strength, (2) origin and development, (3) achievements and failures, (4) demography, that is, the patterns of class, section, religion, and national origin one finds in each, (5) the image that each has of itself, (6) the image that each has of the other, (7) style, if we may use that word to describe the discernible character displayed by each party as it goes about its business, (8) principles and policies, and (9) future prospects. In the hands of these parties we have placed a great deal of responsibility for the conduct of our public business, and they deserve to be better known. One would almost think that there had been a conspiracy of ignorance among the citizens of the United States, so little do we know that is certain—and so much do we know that is wrong—about our two durable parties.

In undertaking this examination of the parties, we must be reasonably clear about which of their several faces we are observing at any given time. The title "Democratic party" or "Republican party" can be used interchangeably to denote one of five fairly distinguishable human groupings, whether at the national, state, or local level, or at all three together:

The *governmental party*, those who have been elected or appointed to office under the party's label (most visible in the legislature).

The *organization*, those who give all or a sizable part of their lives to manning and managing the extragovernmental machinery (most visible in the clubhouses and the conventions).

The *committed electorate*, the loyal, unswerving, "card-carrying" members of the party for whom it is a secular church (most visible at party rallies or on the list of financial contributors).

The *habitual electorate*, those who have a steady record of voting for the party's candidates (most visible in the party's primaries—along with the usual crowd of interlopers).

The *occasional electorate*, all those who voted for the party's candidates, or at least the most important of them, at the last election.

Each of these groupings may be defined as the party, and one who was determined to be more scientific than I (or was unconcerned about being more pedantic) would halt repeatedly to make his identification absolutely clear. I must beg to be excused from this responsibility, trusting that my readers can keep this categorization ready at hand at all times, harking back to it myself only occasionally and under severe pressure. Most of the time the title "Democratic party" or "Republican party" can be understood to stand for the complicated social entity made up of the first four "parties" in this list. Without further apology for vagueness, let me move on to give my own impression of our two great parties.

The Democratic party is first to be saluted, not because it is necessarily the better of the two—every American, after all, must make his own choice in this matter—but because it is unquestionably the older. Indeed, it is so old that some men have called it "venerable." In the length of its years the Democratic party is, of course, only a poor match for the House of Commons and no match at all for the Papacy; but among other human agencies created for the pursuit of man's collective ends it ranks with some of the oldest. Not many governments, constitutions, alliances, fraternal orders, universities, churches, or companies have existed in unbroken course as long as this amazing political organism. It is exactly as old as the American party system, which means that it is by all odds the oldest full-bodied party in the world. The Democrats were a party in every sense of the word when the Whigs and Tories were still clusters of leader-oriented factions or simply political tendencies in the British Parliament.

If it is the oldest of political parties, it is also the toughest. In the course of 160-odd years its death by explosion or attrition has been foretold a dozen times, and still it plods and occasionally skips along the path of political destiny. It plods and skips, be it noted, with considerable success; indeed, its present condition must be described as "flourishing." The compelling fact of American politics today is that the Democratic party is the majority party.[3] The majority is an uneasy one, especially at the point where the South joins suspicious hands with Northern unions and city machines, and it can win victories far more easily than it can do anything with them. Still, it is a majority. All other things being equal, which they are more often than not on the vast, self-adjusting scale of American politics, the Democrats should win every nationwide election. Even when the high volatility of the electorate is taken into full account, the solid Democratic bulge is plainly visible. Well over 60 per cent of American voters who register under a party label are registered as Democrats; well over 55 per cent intend to vote Democratic if they can. Elmo Roper's estimate of "normal voting affiliation," which was arrived at through use of the best techniques that opinion research can muster, gives 50 per cent to the Democrats, 34 per cent to the Republicans, and 16 per cent to the ranks of genuine independence. A more finely shaded analysis of party identification reveals the interesting figures of Table 2.

The majority status of the Democrats shows up clearly in the breakdown of offices currently held by the two parties. The Democrats have an edge of 283 to 154 in the House of

Table 2. Distribution of Respondents in Four National Samples, 1952–1956, according to Strength of Party Identification [4]

Party identification	October 1952	September 1953	October 1954	October 1956
Strong Democrat	22%	22%	22%	21%
Weak Democrat	25	23	25	23
Independent Democrat	10	8	9	6
Independent	5	4	7	9
Independent Republican	7	6	6	8
Weak Republican	14	15	14	14
Strong Republican	13	15	13	15
Apolitical, don't know	4	7	4	4
	100%	100%	100%	100%

Representatives, 65 to 35 in the Senate, 34 to 16 in state governorships, and 32 to 7 in state legislatures (with 9 under split control and 2 nonpartisan). Their margin at the local level, which extends from the city council in New York to the school board in Mount Nebo, West Virginia, is no less commanding. The Democrats, we may conclude, have just about everything—everything, it would seem, except the Presidency, which they lost in 1952 and again in 1956 because personality plays almost as powerful a role as party loyalty in American politics. Of that, more later.

The Democracy, as this party was once fondly known, had its origin in the conflict of economic and sectional interests (and, to a lesser extent, in the conflict of constitutional theories and of personalities) in the first years under the Constitution.[5] It would be hard to say exactly which national election first found the Democrats (or, more exactly, Democratic Republicans) contesting with the Federalists for partisan command of the government; 1800 is perhaps the most acceptable date. By that year the politicians and people who had formed around the person of Thomas Jefferson were a going party in all five senses I mentioned above. Thanks to the old "court-country" cleavage to which John Adams called the attention of posterity, to the catalytic impact of Hamilton's plans for an industrial America, to the suspicions entertained by Virginia planters of the plutocracy of Boston and New York, and to the sharpening differences of opinion about the permissiveness and centripetal force of the new Constitution, the Democratic Republicans were a tendency (the "Republican Interest") in the country from the very beginning, an identifiable group in Congress by 1792, a governmental party by 1795, an election-fighting alliance by 1796, and a visible if loose nationwide organization by 1800.[6] The importance of personality, then as now a mighty force in our politics, can hardly be overestimated. Jefferson, whether reluctant as in 1794–1795 or eager as in 1797–1800, was the kind of leader around whom men, legends, and victorious combinations form and flourish.[7] Madison, whose vital role in the political maneuverings of this decade is just now coming to be fully appreciated,[8] was the skillful architect of the governmental party. Men such as William Branch Giles and Albert Gallatin wrung the last ounce of partisan usefulness out of Jay's Treaty. Men such as Wilson Cary Nicholas and John Breckinridge did the same with the Alien and Sedition Acts. And men such as Aaron Burr, John Beckley, Philip Freneau, George Clinton, James Hutchinson, Gideon Granger, James Monroe, John Francis Mercer, and Thomas McKean did much to build the scatter of republican societies and other local groupings into the organization that scored a historic victory in 1800.

The most remarkable thing about the birth of the Democratic Republicans was the way in which, in anticipation of future generations of Democratic politicians, a party was put together out of discordant interests that were prepared to submerge their differences for the sake of victory over an enemy whom they all disliked even more intensely than they disliked each other. The clasping of hands between Thomas

Jefferson, leader of the rural, agrarian South, and Aaron Burr, leader of the urban, laboring North, was an event of immense consequence for the future of American politics. The bargains they struck, both explicit and implicit, are still the chartered articles of the Democratic party. To maintain the strange and uneasy alliance of planting South and toiling North, of courthouse and city hall, is still the great object of Democratic energies.

The party of Jefferson went forward from 1800 to even more spectacular victories in 1804 and 1808, so spectacular indeed that the party in opposition, the celebrated Federalists, sank into oblivion after the election of 1816, and for a short time the country experienced the strange condition of benevolent one-party rule. In the Era of Good Feelings partisanship declined to a record low and personality rose to a record high as forces in national politics. A healthy democracy, however, is no place for a political monopoly, and America was already too heavily committed to political and social democracy to permit this state of affairs to exist for long. Political monopolies, moreover, have a way of cracking down the middle when pressure is put on them, and the pressures of invention and expansion were already hard at work. The Era of Good Feelings came to an abrupt end in the elections of 1824 and 1828.

Out of these elections and around the person of Andrew Jackson, who had once complained of the "monster called party spirit," arose that combination of economic and sectional interests which has endured to this day as the Democratic party.[9] Out of these elections and around the persons of Daniel Webster and Henry Clay arose that alliance of "shop and till" which endured only to the 1850's as the Whig party. And out of the conflict of Democrats and Whigs emerged the American political system—complete with such features as two major parties, a sprinkle of third parties, national nominating conventions, state and local bosses, patronage, popular campaigning, and the Presidency as the focus of politics. There are political historians (mostly Republicans, I suspect) who argue that the Democracy of Jackson was a brand-new party, but there were too many personal, emotional, and organizational ties between the Democratic Republicans of 1820 and the Democrats of 1830 to permit us to agree. The party of Jefferson neither died nor faded away. It grew fat and happy with success, split violently in the manner of many fat and happy parties, was captured by the largest of its components, and emerged from its ordeal as the tough, confident, self-conscious legatee of the political Jefferson. All things considered, especially the shattering effects of this age of rapid transition upon all the nation's values and habits, the new Democracy was a remarkably faithful projection of the old, which was what such skilled makers as Martin Van Buren and Thomas Hart Benton intended it to be.

The Democratic party, born anew if not born again, moved forward from 1830 to become and remain the most powerful single political force in American history. Like all institutions and all men, it has had its ups and downs. It has known glory under such as Andrew Jackson and Franklin D. Roosevelt, greatness under such as James K. Polk and Harry S. Truman, mediocrity under such as Franklin Pierce and Alton B. Parker, frustration under such as Martin Van Buren and Grover Cleveland, despair under such as Stephen A. Douglas and James M. Cox. It has scraped the stars with Woodrow Wilson and Adlai Stevenson; it has wallowed in the mud with William Marcy Tweed, Edward H. Crump, and Theodore ("The Man") Bilbo. It has displayed shrewdness and stupidity, farsightedness and blindness, courage and cowardice, moral fiber and amoral callousness. It has shocked the fastidious, discomfited the established, comforted the disinherited, and amused the detached. It has been, in short, an American party operating at full blast on the American scene.

If we can rise above petty detail and see our history in broadest outline, we can give the Democratic party more than modest praise for at least nine grand achievements, more than pardonable blame for five grand failures. These are, of course, in addition to the triumphs (or failures) for which we give credit (or blame) to the whole party system, that is, to the two old parties in fairly equal amounts. The achievements of the Democrats, by which I mean Good Things that happened to the United States because they initiated them or pushed them or at least speeded their inevitable coming, were (1) the easy acceptance of the ground rules of the Constitution and the prudent use of the powers it delegates, all this under Jefferson and Madison; (2) the infusion into the American body politic of huge but fortunately not lethal doses of populism under Jackson; (3) the long stand against disunion, narrowly selfish in motive but enormously effective in result, under Polk, Pierce, and Douglas; (4) the reluctant reunion of North and South after the Civil War; (5) the reintroduction of at least a measure of integrity to the national government under Cleveland; (6) the sharpening of the national conscience under Bryan—and under the prodding of the Populists; (7) the Americanization of millions of immigrants in the flooded years between 1840 and 1920; (8) the facing-up to the new responsibilities of government for social welfare and economic health under Wilson and then Roosevelt; and (9) the simultaneous facing-up to the new responsibilities of diplomacy in a shrinking, agitated world under the same men and Harry S. Truman.

The failures of the Democrats, by which I mean the Bad Things for which they were primarily to blame, were (1) the introduction of the "spoils system" (an event, to be sure, with healthy as well as unhealthy consequences) and its expansion into a hydra of inefficiency and corruption; (2) the attrition of the process of purposeful compromise within the party that led inexorably to Sumter and Bull Run; (3) the postwar debasement of political morals well below the natural level of American conduct, especially through the practices of the city machines; (4) the absence of political and moral capacity to check the upsurge of the spirit of plunder under the Republicans in the 1870's and 1880's; and (5) the generally shallow, shortsighted performance—except in the demanding years under Wilson—between 1900 and 1932. Into the production of this catalogue of success and failure I have put, admittedly and necessarily, a healthy measure of subjectivity, but I think it would be approved, in outline if not in every detail, by a stout majority of American historians. The Democrats, I repeat, have had their ups and downs.

The obverse of the compelling fact of American politics is that the Republican party is the minority party. All other things being equal, which they were in 1954 and 1958 and were not in 1952 and 1956, the Republicans should lose every nationwide election. They are the party upon which that solid Democratic bulge presses constantly. They cannot register more than 40 per cent of American voters and cannot count on more than 33 per cent to stand fast against temptation. They are outnumbered by almost 2 to 1 in the House and Senate, by a full 2 to 1 in the state legislatures, and by better than 2 to 1 in the governors' mansions. Even outside the South the margin against them is 7 to 5 in the upper houses, 4 to 3 in the lower houses, and 8 to 5 in the governors' mansions. They took a fearful licking in 1958; they have few substantial hopes of capturing the House and none of capturing the Senate in 1960. And yet their spirits are high and their minds full of plans, for they have the one wonderful thing the Democrats lack—the Presidency. It would be hard to overestimate the immense satisfaction the Republican party draws from the sight of one of its own men in the White House, where none but "scheming, spendthrift, wrongheaded Democrats" lived for the "twenty long years" from 1933 to 1953. Dwight D. Eisenhower has been many things to the Republicans—a world-renowned leader, a popular idol (the first such Republican since Theodore Roosevelt), a benevolent father image, a willing dispenser of patronage, a peacemaker among the party's squabbling wings—but most of all he has been a winner, and a winner is what a minority party must have from time to time lest it sink into a state of demoralized torpor. The mere presence of Eisenhower in the White House is enough to smother the Republican party's own special urge to fly apart, and more than enough to inspire its faithful workers to move into the battle of 1960 with quick and confident step. If the party can win the Presidency at least half the time, why cry over the House of Representatives and a handful of state governorships?

The Republicans have not always been a minority party. Through most of their history they have lived in the comforting knowledge that a majority of voting Americans gave first allegiance to them. They are, of course, the third major party to arise and do battle with the enduring Democrats. The first was the Federalists, a reluctant political force that burst upon the scene along with the Democrats and then sank into oblivion in less than twenty years. The most important causes of its early demise—all of them object lessons to future opponents of the Democrats—were that it was a nativist party in a land already beginning to fill up with immigrants; an antipopular party in a land over which political and social democracy was sweeping in great waves; an uncompromising party, a group of men anxious only to load more favors on the favored and unable therefore to lure new elements into a coalition; a faction-ridden party that made no attempt to hide or heal its wounds; and a reluctant party, one that had trouble thinking of itself as a party at all and that was neither ideologically nor organizationally nor tactically prepared to submit to the imperatives of politics in a constitutional democracy. As Denis Brogan has written, "The Old Federalists had been more of the temper of Coriolanus; even when they wooed the plebs, they did it ungracefully and unconvincingly." [10] An American party must woo the plebs wholeheartedly or go out of business.

The second party to oppose the Democrats was the Whigs,

an eager political force that arose out of the wreckage of the Era of Good Feelings, coalesced in savage reaction to the person and program of Andrew Jackson, contested its first national election in 1832 (as the National Republicans), and contested its last one as a major party in 1852. If the Federalists died because they were much too reluctant to obey "the unwritten laws of American politics," the Whigs died because they were much too willing, as they proved in their wonderfully mawkish campaign of 1840. They were, indeed, the coalition to end all coalitions, a patchwork party with few premonitions of immortality, a loose alliance of every section and interest, which was sure to crack under the first hard blow. That blow was delivered by Stephen A. Douglas in January 1854 with his introduction of the Kansas-Nebraska Bill and consequent reopening of the slavery issue, and within a few months the Whigs had disappeared as an effective force in American politics. Within the same few months two new forces had emerged—one, the nativist Know-Nothing party, which contested the elections of 1854 and 1856 and then, happily, disappeared; the other, the Republican party, which also contested these elections and then, happily, went on to glory in 1860.

There are four facts about the birth and infancy of the Republican party which it is essential for us to have in mind. First, this party was the product of a truly spontaneous eruption of political sentiment. No one town can be called its birthplace, although both Ripon, Wisconsin, and Jackson, Michigan, have cases worth shouting about. No one man served as the real or symbolic catalyst of the forces that went into it. It had no Washington or Jefferson, no Madison or Hamilton, no Clay or Jackson. It was, indeed, the most powerful, authentic grass-roots movement in American political history. Second, that sentiment was essentially sectional in origin and appeal. By making their first stand a bold one against the extension of slavery in the territories, the Re-

publicans, in effect, tossed away the South, and to this day
they live with the knowledge that they have never been a
fully national party. Third, that sentiment was essentially
progressive, democratic, even radical; the party itself was
based as much on ideals as on interests. Whatever the Republicans were to become in later years, they were far from
being a conservative, business-oriented party in infancy. The
very name Republican was a salute to the Jeffersonian
heritage, and Washington and Jefferson ("the first Free-
Soiler") were the only two patron saints acclaimed in the
party's first platform. (In these same years the name of Jefferson was conspicuously absent from Democratic platforms.)
Finally, the Republicans drew their leaders and gathered their
voters from almost every party and group on the American
scene—from the Whigs, yes, but also from the Democrats,
Free-Soilers, Abolitionists, Know-Nothings, local third parties,
and, lest we forget, the temperance movement. Lincoln's great
Cabinet, an artfully constructed political alliance, bears wit-
ness to the motley origins of the Republicans:

President: Lincoln, an Illinois Whig.

Vice-President: Hannibal Hamlin, a Maine Democrat.

Secretary of State: William H. Seward, a "conscience
Whig" from New York.

Secretary of Treasury: Salmon P. Chase of Ohio, succes-
sively in the Whig, Liberty-Abolitionist, Free-Soil, Democrat,
and Know-Nothing ranks.

Secretary of War: Simon Cameron, Democratic boss of
Pennsylvania.

Secretary of the Navy: Gideon Welles, a tried-and-true
Connecticut Democrat.

Postmaster-General: Montgomery Blair of Missouri and
Maryland, a throwback to Jacksonian Democracy.

Attorney-General: Edward Bates, a Missouri Whig who
went right on calling himself a Whig.

Secretary of the Interior: Caleb Smith, an Indiana Whig.[11]

Motley and populist in origin, the Republicans became more like-minded and conservative in power—conservative, that is to say, except when they dealt with the South. After a rocketing start toward dominance under Lincoln and Grant, the party fell into a neck-and-neck struggle with the resurgent Democrats between 1876 and 1896. These twenty years were the only period in American history during which the natural, two-way division of our politics struck an even balance. For eighteen of those years the Republicans held the Senate; for sixteen the Democrats held the House. In all five presidential elections the winner's margin in the popular vote was paper-thin. Indeed, in two elections (1876 and 1888) he had no margin at all.

The bitter fight between McKinley and Bryan marked the coming of a new era in American politics, and from then until 1932, or even a few years after that, the Republicans were the majority party in the government and in the country. In all these years the Democrats placed only one man, Woodrow Wilson, in the Presidency—the first time (1912) because of a savage split in the Republican party, the second time (1916) by the skin of Wilson's prominent teeth. The golden age of the Republicans was inaugurated in Warren G. Harding's fantastic victory in 1920, the dark ages in Herbert Hoover's demoralizing defeat in 1932. That defeat was still another watershed in American politics, for Franklin Roosevelt seized the main chance offered him by history and put together the new coalition that holds sway, precarious but consequential, to this day. For nearly thirty years the Republicans have been, in Samuel Lubell's metaphor, the moon in orbit around the Democratic sun.[12] At one point, indeed, the moon was in virtual eclipse. From the election of 1936 the Republicans emerged with 8 votes out of 531 in the electoral college, 17 seats out of 96 in the Senate, 89 seats out of 435 in the House, and 8 governors out of 48 in the states. Yet despite widespread predictions of an early death, the Republicans—

thanks to a hard core of like-minded interests, to state parties that would not lie down and die, to the visible cracks in the Roosevelt majority, and to the memories of better days—rose again to wage stern battle in 1940, a winning battle in 1946, and an all-winning campaign in 1952. The Republicans, it seems, are here to stay.

Those memories hark back to seventy-five years of service to the nation through service principally to its productive classes. Once again I speak subjectively and yet as the interpreter of scholarly consensus when I list these as the grand achievements of the Republican party: (1) the creation, after the two aborted attempts of the Federalists and Whigs, of a legitimate, viable alternative to the enduring Democracy; (2) the forcing of the slavery issue, which had to be forced sooner or later if America was to live in good conscience among the civilized nations of the world; (3) the preservation of the Union, which was a historic enough achievement all by itself to justify the Republicans for generations to come; (4) the fertilization (if that is the proper word) of American enterprise in the late nineteenth century; and (5) the acceptance, none too soon but also not too late, of the burdens of the New Economy and the New Internationalism in the middle of the twentieth century.

If this catalogue of achievements is shorter and less impressive than that displayed by the Democrats, this could well be because the Republicans are sixty years younger and six degrees more conservative. In all fairness one must also give the Republicans some credit for the brilliant solo performances of such mavericks as Theodore Roosevelt, George W. Norris, and Hiram Johnson, and of such premature internationalists as Henry L. Stimson, Charles Evans Hughes, and Elihu Root. Under the loose rules of American politics the more conservative of our two parties may properly take a bow for the applause directed toward its troublemakers. Its lowest bow, however, should be for the applause it gets as a party at least as successful as the other party in fulfilling its peculiar mission. The Republicans of the last half-century have been as good a conserving party as the Democrats have been an innovating party, which may or may not be saying much.

The failures of the Republicans are paradoxically and inextricably intertwined with their achievements. I would mention three: (1) they solved the slavery issue, and in the only way in which the South would finally permit it to be solved, yet they went on to disregard Lincoln's advice and to pursue a policy of vengeance in the Reconstruction period; (2) they fertilized American industry liberally, yet far too many of the fruits ended up in the pockets of the few and far too few in the hands of the many; and (3) they acted the part of the conservative governing party at a time, the 1920's, when America had moved with bewildering speed into an entirely new situation at home and abroad, and they were quite unprepared to deal effectively with the breakdown of the old order in either area. The memory of a feckless Harding, a motionless Coolidge, and a whipsawed Hoover will be with the American electorate for some time to come. The ghost of the Great Depression, for which the Republicans are rightly held to a good share of the blame, is a hard one to lay.

A party is something more than an organization or a legend or a record. It is a multitude of people, and if it cannot count them in the millions it is not a party of any consequence on the American scene. We must now talk of the Democrats and Republicans as people, millions of people. In particular, we must take honest account of the historic tendency of Americans to swear allegiance to one party or to the other on the basis of such factors as section, race, and class, and of the historic tendency of one party or the other to grant easier access to power and privilege to those men who bear the right sectional, racial, and class credentials.

This is, let us be forewarned, a tricky approach to the study of American politics. To speak of "the Irish vote" or "the farm vote" or even "the egghead vote" is to speak of real individuals as an abstract mass, and thus to fall easy prey to misleading assumptions about the workings of our democracy. It is to foster the illusion of great blocs of voters standing fast in the ancient ways or swinging massively from one party to another, to minimize the importance of personal choice and prejudice in the political process, and to skim over the stubborn fact that any one American appears in at least a dozen different guises in the neat tables of statistics with which political demographers like to play. Martin O'Toole of Boston, Massachusetts, may be both a self-conscious Irishman and a self-conscious Democrat, but how can we be sure that there is a one-to-one relationship between his descent and his politics, especially when we know that he is also fifty years old, a male, a college graduate, a Roman Catholic, a New Englander, an urban dweller, a homeowner, a self-employed businessman, a veteran, a Rotarian, and the son of a father who, out of gnawing dislike of his in-laws, the O'Shaughnessys, always voted Republican? And how, in any case, are we to establish his allegiance, especially when we learn that he split his ticket in 1952 and again in 1956? Where is a man most likely to exhibit his true political colors: in presidential, congressional, state, or local elections? Some of the best studies in political demography in recent years are gently misleading, for the interviews from which they drew their data were focused exclusively on presidential elections, and such elections always find American voters in a perverse and volatile mood. Yet who can say that a study based upon a congressional or state or local election, even one in which all extraneous factors seemed to cancel one another out, would be any more accurate or reliable?

Having dutifully entered all these disclaimers, I still think we have a right to speak of demographic influences on preference, choice, and behavior in American politics. Thanks to careful students of our voting habits such as Elmo Roper, Angus Campbell, and Paul Lazarsfeld, we know a good deal more about these influences than we did only ten years ago, and we are accumulating more data all the time. Never will we be able to speak with scientific certainty about why men vote the way they do, but already we can speak with confidence about observed tendencies of men to vote one way or another—or not to vote at all—because of various forces that help to shape their lives. Let me call attention to nine such forces that have a visible influence on the voting habits of the American electorate: section, locale, class, calling, ethnology, religion, age, education, and sex.

At one time in our history *sectionalism* was the decisive factor in American politics. Each of the parties had a solid base in certain sections of the country; the political life of many states was a virtual monopoly of one party; voters in these states had a comfortable habit of going down the line for the majority party. One was a declared Republican in Vermont, Pennsylvania, Kansas, or eastern Tennessee, or one had to do a considerable amount of explaining. One was a birthright Democrat in South Carolina, Alabama, Texas, or western Tennessee, or one could not save himself from disrepute with the best explanation in the world. Sections, in V. O. Key's phrase, were the "building blocks for the American parties." Each party concentrated on putting together "intersectional combinations powerful enough to govern"; [13] national elections were often won and lost on the perverse basis of sectional pride or disaffection. In most one-party states politics was a depressing affair exhibiting a fat and complacent majority party, a desiccated and feckless minority party (with almost a vested interest in defeat), and a political life distinguished chiefly by apathy and petty corruption.[14] In the nation at large the urges and prejudices of sectionalism were the first concern of all leading politicians.

In politics as in most other areas of American life the trend in recent years has been away from sectional variety and (by way, paradoxically, of the growth of new varieties) toward national unity. Elections to the Presidency or Congress "are increasingly won and lost by influences felt throughout the land." [15] The Democrats can now make a real contest of every important election in every state of the Union. The Republicans, though cut off by memory and vested interest from the courthouses and statehouses of the old Confederacy, have at least the outlines of a "presidential party" in most of those eleven states.

Yet section is still a force in American national politics and a key to the political habits of large groups of persons who might otherwise be expected to vote the other way.[16] The South is still solid for the Democracy in local, state, and congressional elections, and it would like to be solid in presidential elections. Northern New England, the Western Reserve, and the upper Mississippi Valley are still more Republican than Democratic; southern New England,[17] the Far West (except Oregon), and the Border (for example, Kentucky and Oklahoma) are more Democratic than Republican. And that wonder of American politics, the "mountain Republicans" of the South, are still very much a footnote to all tables of statistics that demonstrate the solidarity of that section. If one wishes to walk among the stanchest Republicans in America, let him turn away from Orange County in Vermont or Westchester County in New York and go to Owsley and Jackson counties in Kentucky, Sevier and Johnson counties in Tennessee, Mitchell County in North Carolina, Winston County in Alabama, and Gillespie and Kendall counties in Texas. Here he will find the sons and grandsons of men who detested the Confederacy; here he will find majorities (for instance, in Jackson County, Kentucky) of 89 per cent for Alf M. Landon, 89 per cent for Thomas E. Dewey, and 89 per cent for Dwight D. Eisenhower. And here, as in Vermont and Kansas and above all Mississippi and Georgia, he will find evidence that sectional pride or purpose remains a decisive influence on political allegiance in the United States. "Vote as you shot!" was the battle cry of the Grand Army of the Republic, and millions of Americans are still voting as their grandfathers shot one hundred years ago.

So true is this of the eleven states of the old Confederacy that much of what I have to say in the next few pages about the influence of locale or calling or religion, especially in shaping the Democratic party, is simply not applicable to the South. To almost every statement I make about that incredible party the reader is begged to append a footnote reading either "outside the South" or, with apologies to Stephen Potter, "but not in the South." I will deal directly with the problem of the South in good time.

A related influence in shaping political preference is *locale*, that is, residence in one of the natural habitats of the American people: city, suburb, and rural area. Each of these habitats is a clearly distinguishable social phenomenon; each has a characteristic political style that rubs off on a majority of the persons who live in it. I do not want to oversimplify the residential pattern of our politics, yet I think it safe to say that those who live in cities are more likely to be Democrats than Republicans, those who live outside them are more likely to be Republicans than Democrats.

The cities of America have been, with a few conspicuous exceptions, Democratic strongholds since time out of mind. New York City went strongly for Jefferson in 1800, and New York City will go strongly for any candidate the Democrats are likely to put up in 1960. This may well be because New York, like most cities, has a larger share of low-income, foreign-born, laboring persons, but it is also because there is a natural, time-tested affinity between the restless Democratic party and the restless city. This affinity is growing stronger, and the urban-rural antagonisms in our politics, of which Alfred E. Smith was the unwitting chief craftsman in modern times, will persist as a major force both in and out of our national and state legislatures.

The long-range shift in the balance of population from country to city gave the Democrats their opportunity to supplant the Republicans as the majority party. Franklin D. Roosevelt and his colleagues, taking heart from Smith's lead, seized this opportunity so boldly that even today, years after his death, the "big-city masses" stand "like a human wall between the Republicans and their past dominance." [18] There are dozens of reliable sets of statistics that could be used to illustrate this Democratic ascendancy in our large cities, but surely the most convincing has to do with urban representation in the House of Representatives. Fifteen cities in the United States (excluding Washington and all Southern cities) count more than 500,000 inhabitants. From within the boundaries of these cities, that is, from constituencies that are wholly urban in site, come 65 congressmen; 55 of these representatives of urban America are Democrats, ten are Republicans. So far as I can tell, all but two of the Republicans come from a section of a city (like Queens in New York) that is more suburban than urban in character and interest. The big cities are Democratic, and so are a majority of the middle-sized cities. The pattern of Democratic ascendancy is repeated with few changes in Newark, Seattle, Providence, Gary, and most of the rest.

Rural America outside the South is almost as Republican as urban America is Democratic. One must account for this fact, too, in terms of many cultural and historic forces, but again there can be no doubt of a natural, time-tested affinity, in this instance between the slower pace of the Republicans and the slower pace of our small towns.[19] The country always seems to react to the existence of the city more violently than does the city to the country, and it seems certain that a conscious distrust of the urban masses and their strange political ways had much to do with the creation of a Republican hegemony—and of a virtual identification of Republicanism and respectability

—in the county seats and on the farms of rural America.

In recent years Americans have flocked by the millions into a third habitat, the suburb. There are suburbs and suburbs strewn around the cities of America, and it is dangerous to generalize too glibly about the politics of these rookeries. Still, it is a fact, whether attested in Bronxville or Shaker Heights or Park Forest or Silver Spring, that the suburbs of America are predominantly Republican. It is not at all certain that people who move out of New York to New Rochelle or out of Boston to Wellesley are converted by the mere fact of passage from Democrats to Republicans.[20] Men move from the city and change their politics (if they change at all) out of the same

Table 3. Percentage of Republican State Plurality
Cast by Suburbs [21]

	In 1920	In 1952
Philadelphia suburbs	8	52
New York suburbs	8	44
Chicago suburbs	7	40

impulse, which is most commonly a rise in occupation, income, status, and aspiration. It is certain that they tend to vote Republican when they get there, and that they have now got there in numbers that are almost, but not quite, decisive in our political process. Robert Wood points out that in 1955 "five million of New York's thirteen million residents were in the suburbs and two million of Chicago's total of six million. In Los Angeles, suburbanites outnumbered central city residents three to two; in Boston the ratio was two to one; in Pittsburgh almost three to one; and elsewhere the gap was closing. One out of every four Americans was a suburbanite." [22] Lubell confirms both the Republicanism and the importance of the suburbs in Tables 3 and 4.

Table 4. A Profile of Class Solidarity [23]

| | Per cent Republican | | |
	1936	1948	1952
New York			
Vote in city	24	35	44
Nearby suburbs	54	66	69
Philadelphia			
Vote in city	37	48	41
Nearby suburbs	52	64	63
Cleveland			
Vote in city	30	35	40
Nearby suburbs	54	62	63
Chicago			
Vote in city	33	41	45
Nearby suburbs	50	64	66
Los Angeles			
Vote in city	28	42	52
Nearby suburbs	36	51	59

"A profile of class solidarity"—that seems like a rather harsh title for Lubell to paste on Table 4. Harsh, yes, but also honest, for there can be little doubt that the sharpening urban-suburban cleavage in our mid-century politics is a product of difference in status rather than in residence or tradition. *Class* is a dirty word in the American vocabulary, yet to deny the existence of well-defined social classes in this country would be dishonest, to deny their importance for politics would be fatuous. The fact is that class has now become the most important single force in shaping the political behavior of Americans and that, consequently, class is the most reliable single index to political allegiance. Again I am oversimplifying the dimensions of one force and ignoring the influence of many others, including personal choice based on rational principles, but it is well understood that the higher is a man's perch on the

many-staged, well-traveled ladder of the American class structure, the more likely is he to be a Republican—and a conscious,
committed, voting, contributing Republican at that. This has
been true of our politics, I might add, for a long time. James
Bryce noted in the 1880's that the Republicans were

the party in whose ranks respectable, steady, pious, well-conducted
men are to be looked for. If you find yourself dining with one of
"the best people" in any New England city, or in Philadelphia, or
in Cincinnati, Cleveland, Chicago, or Minneapolis, you assume that
the guest sitting next you is a Republican, almost as confidently as
in English county society you would assume your neighbour to be
a Tory; that is to say, you may sometimes be wrong, but in four
cases out of five you will be right. . . . It is in that party you look
to find . . . the men of substance who desire to see things go on
quietly, with no shocks given to business confidence by rash legislation.[24]

The disposition of the upper levels of American society
toward the Republicans—or should we say away from the
Democrats?—is even stronger and more self-conscious today.
If we can accept, with the usual reservations, Lloyd Warner's
six-staged ladder,[25] the pattern of political allegiance in an
average community would appear to be:

Class	Per cent of population (*very rough*)	Per cent voting Republican (*even rougher*)
Upper upper	2	85+
Lower upper	3	85+
Upper middle	15	75+
Lower middle	35	50
Upper lower	30	40−
Lower lower	15	30−

I trust that my readers will not try to find too much in this
table, which raises ten questions for every one it answers. The
one that it does answer justifies it fully, and that is the question
of class as a determinant of (and index to) party allegiance. The

answer—the preponderance of Republican sentiment above the middle line of the American class structure and of Democratic sentiment below it—is one to which no one of us can henceforth close his eyes. This is especially true because, according to recent studies, there appears to be a high degree of perception among Americans of all classes of the facts I have brought forward: that there are indeed classes in this country, that most men are aware of their own class level, and that most men recognize the Republicans as the party of the upper and upper-middle classes and the Democrats as the party of the lower and lower-middle classes.[26] The short title for the former classes is "the rich," for the latter "the poor."

The increasing political importance of class position, whether objectively occupied or subjectively perceived, is demonstrated convincingly in the South. Most of the influences with which we are dealing in this chapter work only ineffectually in the South, blunted as they are by the overpowering impact of sectionalism on the whole political process. Class, however, appears to tell, not merely in the shaping of factions to contest for ascendancy within the Democracy, but in the creation of what was, in effect, a two-party South in the presidential elections of 1952 and 1956. Most of the votes for Eisenhower were polled in the upper reaches of the social order, most of those for Stevenson in the lower reaches, both white and colored. Lubell reported his own discovery of this cleavage in tables such as Tables 5, 6, and 7.

This should be evidence enough to support the hypothesis (or, more honestly, to prove the fact) that American politics, like the politics of other countries, is disposed to break along class lines. The lines, fortunately, are still blurred, and we are far from a politics in which class is not merely an influence but an imperative. As Charles A. Beard observed more than forty years ago, it is not wealth but "the center of gravity of wealth" that is "on the Republican side," not poverty but "the center of gravity of poverty" that is "on the Democratic side." [27] The

Table 5. Percentage for Eisenhower by Economic Class [28]

City	Negro precincts	Labor precincts	Silk-stocking precincts
Mobile, Ala.	11	34	72
Jacksonville, Fla.	13	28	79
Miami, Fla.	24	56	78
Tampa, Fla.	23	49	62
Atlanta, Ga.	25	28	67
Augusta, Ga.	23	40	75
New Orleans, La.	10	56	73
Baton Rouge, La.	5	36	64
Greensboro, N.C.	7	44	64
Charlotte, N.C.	7	39	82
Houston, Tex.	5	37	87
Dallas, Tex.	10	44	85
Richmond, Va.	15	43	75
13-city average	12	39	75

Table 6. Democratic Percentage for President in Houston Precincts Ranked by Average Home Valuation [29]

Average valuation	1936	1940	1944	1948	1952
Over $30,000	57	29	18	7	6
$19,000	71	47	35	29	13
$15,000	81	58	50	25	22
$13,000	79	60	52	23	22
$10,000	86	74	64	33	26
$ 9,000	90	80	68	40	33
$ 8,000	93	85	79	61	50
$ 7,000	93	88	78	57	49
$ 5,000	94	89	84	66	60
Under $5,000	91	89	87	72	60

Table 7. Economic Voting in New Orleans [30]

Economic class	Number of precincts Eisenhower won	Number of such precincts in city
Upper income	32	32
Low upper	3	4
Middle income	89	115
Low middle	5	11
Low income	6	126
Totals	135	288

Republicans can count on at least one vote in every three cast by those at the bottom of the American social structure. The Democrats would hardly know what to do without the sprinkling of aristocrats—men of manners, education, old wealth, and perhaps bad consciences—who tone up the party, keep it out of debt, and provide candidates for the Presidency. The evil day of the class struggle in politics is still remote in most parts of America.

Calling is, in most senses, just another word for class, yet it, too, can be isolated and treated as an influence on political allegiance. In the light of what we know already, it should come as no surprise to learn that most businessmen, whether large or small, are Republicans, most workingmen, whether organized or unorganized, are Democrats, and most farmers, whether in wheat or corn, are Republicans who will vote Democratic at the drop of a parity check.

If the Republican party may be said to have a center of gravity, it is today, as it has been since the 1860's, the business community, the men who manage, advise, supervise, finance, and sell the products of American industry. The Republican party is many parties, but first of all it is "the party of business," and businessmen and their allies rally to its support with a consistency that is rare in American politics. A *Fortune*-sponsored inquiry into the presidential preferences of 1,700 business executives in October 1959 revealed 76 per cent for Nixon, 11 per cent for Rockefeller, and a shriveled 13 per cent willing to support any of the available Democrats. Outside the South, and even inside it for presidential elections, the Republicans can usually count on the votes of roughly 85 per cent of top management, 75 per cent of middle management, and 65 per cent of independent businessmen. At the top of the heap they can count on dollars, too, as Table 8 proves.

Table 8. Division between Republican and Democratic Campaigns of Yield of Reported Contributions of $500 or More in 1956 from Officers and Directors of Types of Business Enterprises [31]

Type of enterprise	Republican	Democratic
225 largest corporations	94.6%	5.4%
29 largest oil companies	95.9	4.1
10 leading radio and TV stations	97.4	2.6
17 certified airlines	80.7	19.3
37 advertising agencies	100.0	0.0
47 underwriters of bonds	99.2	0.8

If some of our large corporations had their way, the businessmen who serve them would rally to Republicanism with fervor as well as with consistency. There has been much talk in recent years of the importance of "political action" on the part of corporation executives, especially those in the ranks of middle management. The talk in public is necessarily neutral in tone, but there is no doubt that the action called for is action on the Republican front. While General Electric, Ford, Gulf Oil, and Republic Steel are to be commended for encouraging young executives to engage in political activity, they would stop encouraging them in a hurry if more than a token amount of the activity were devoted to electing Democrats to office.[32]

The Democratic party has never been content with less than two centers of gravity, but surely the one with the strongest pull today is organized labor. In many parts of the country it is more correct than misleading to describe the Democrats as a "labor party," and in large parts of one state at least, Governor Williams' Michigan, the bureaucracy of union labor has taken over the functions of the party organization. The men in the ranks of organized labor are neither so enthusiastic nor so Democratic as their leaders would like them to be, and many of the wives of these men have demonstrated an admirable determination to make their own political decisions.[33] Still, even in the presidential elections of 1952 and 1956—the nadir of the Democratic party of this generation—a full 60 per cent of union members voted for Stevenson.[34] In the congressional elections of 1958 the number voting Democratic may have risen to 70 per cent. The working force in America is not quite so heavily committed to the Democrats as the business community is to the Republicans, but the commitment is apparently heavy and persistent enough to push more and more corporations back into active politics. There are, to be sure, a lot more workingmen than businessmen in America, but Republicans are able to live cheerfully with this fact because of three considerations: the three workers in ten who always vote Republican and the added one who can be persuaded to; the failure of the Democrats to reach many wives and relatives of union men; and the generally lower turnout of workers as opposed to businessmen.

The historic allegiance of American farmers is to the Republican party. "Iowa will go Democratic," Senator Dolliver once promised, "the year Hell goes Methodist." His promise was made fifty years ago, however, and Iowa has gone Democratic (if not Hell Methodist) more often than not since 1932, with the help of many farmers whose fathers were straight-out Republicans. That historic allegiance may never quite recover from the shock and strain of the 1930's. Two-party politics is here to stay in parts of America where for generations a Republican was "the thing to be." This two-party cleavage, it appears, is almost as much a matter of status and substance as it is in the cities and suburbs, and the cleavage exists in the small towns as well as in the open spaces of rural America.* The most notable fact about the so-called "farm vote" today is not that it is a two-party vote or that it still leans slightly toward the Republicans, but that increasing numbers of farmers are suspended in the independent middle, ready to move one way or the other with the prevailing wind—or would it be against it? [36] The farmers of America, who have more to get directly from government than does any other major group in the country except the Negroes, are generally credited these days with a special capacity for deliberate, rational choice of candidates. As they have more to get, so they seem to get more, and one reason must surely be their political restlessness. Coyness is often paid off as well as loyalty in the American political system.

Ethnology, a word in which I mean to include both *national origin* and *race*, is a demographic force that is especially difficult to isolate and measure. Can we really say that a city-bred, laboring, Roman Catholic Irishman in Boston votes Democratic primarily because he is Irish, or that a country-bred, small-farming, Protestant German in Wisconsin votes Republican primarily because he is German? And how Irish is an "Irishman" a hundred years from Wexford, or how German a "German" a hundred years from Thuringia? Plainly much nonsense has been written about the ethnic vote in America. Yet it would only compound this nonsense to deny that there is such a vote, or rather many such votes. Although the ethnic factor is not so crucial as it was three or four decades ago, it is important and explosive enough to make politicians handle it with care. It is important because it can hold steady for one or the other party in even the toughest times, explosive because it can be turned inside-out by issues or events that leave other demo-

---

* Lubell has called attention to the fact that, in Iowa at least, "the mainstay of Republican strength in the countryside" may have been "the small town which serviced the farmer" rather than the farmer himself, "the man on Main Street rather than the man with the hoe." [35]

graphic influences in normal balance. Almost every election attests to the importance of ethnology; the election of 1940 attests to its explosiveness. Franklin Roosevelt's best gains over 1936 were scored among voters of Polish, Jewish, and Yankee descent, many of whom looked back across the water and the years to peoples assaulted by Hitler. His heaviest losses were registered among voters of Italian, Irish, and German descent, many of whom gagged at the prospect of a war, side-by-side with Britain, against Germany and Italy.[37]

It is hard to be precise about such matters, since pockets of contradiction have existed all over this country, but the traditional allegiance of major ethnic and racial groups seems to have gone as follows: to the Republicans—the old stock of England, Scotland, and Wales, along with the Germans, Scandinavians, and Negroes; to the Democrats—the new stock generally, beginning with the Irish and coming down through the Poles, Slavs, Italians, and Jews. The Republicans have been, as it were, an American party, the Democrats—outside the South (we must remember always to chime in with "outside the South")—an immigrant party. This is, to be sure, less true today than a generation ago, and it is becoming less true all the time.[38] The urge of most immigrants has been to be accepted as Americans, and acceptance has meant Republicanism, often from the start, for millions of immigrants and their children. The Irish, in particular, have been moving rapidly toward two-party politics based on variations in class and locale, although one would never suspect it as he ran his eye down the long list of Irish names in the chairmanship of the Democratic National Committee. Roper came up with these revealing figures in a survey of the political preferences of voters of Irish descent in the 1952 election: [39]

	Eisenhower	*Stevenson*
Upper income	85%	15%
Lower middle income	55	45
Low income	29	71

The Italians, on the other hand, are perhaps more Democratic than they were in the old days in Providence, Boston, and New York when many of them offered allegiance to the Republican party out of dislike of the Irish. Whatever else he may be, Carmine De Sapio is a major figure in the symbolism of American politics as the first man of Italian descent to be leader of Tammany Hall. It seems almost certain that men with Italian, Jewish, and Polish names will soon be as numerous as the Farleys and Fitzgeralds in the command posts of many of the great city machines. The Democrats of Chicago, the party of "Hinky Dink" Kenna and "Bath House John" Coughlin, had a leader named Jake Arvey even before the Democrats of Manhattan, the party of "Big Tim" Sullivan and "Blue-eyed Billy" Sheehan, had their De Sapio. When the Democrats of Boston, the party of "the Purple Shamrock" and "Honey Fitz" Fitzgerald, put their destiny in the hands of Casimir Pulaski, that, as the sports-writers say, will be "the end of an era."

The two most interesting ethnic groups in American politics today are the Jews and the Negroes, both of which used to vote Republican, both of which now lean heavily—the latter almost too heavily—toward the Democratic party. The Jewish vote is not a large one, but it is alert, active, and self-conscious, and it makes up nearly 25 per cent of the electorate in our four largest cities. The significant and, I think, admirable thing about this vote is that it tends to ignore considerations of status and income. Jews, it would seem, are far more prepared than almost any other identifiable group or interest to rise above such considerations and to cast their votes on emotional or ideological grounds. The political Jew, only loosely tied to his pocketbook, makes a refreshing contrast to the political farmer. Jews cast their votes, be it noted, in a fairly steady 3:1 ratio for the Democratic party. The memory of Franklin Roosevelt combines with a natural liberalism and internationalism to make them one of the rocks of the new Democracy. They ask very little of government, again in contrast to many other groups, and their high level of interest and participation seems to stem in considerable part from a rational understanding of the duties of the good citizen in a democracy.[40] It may also stem, as S. M. Lipset suggests, from "their sensitivity to ethnic discrimination and their lack of effective social intercourse with the upper-status groups in America." [41]

Negroes, on the other hand, have more to get from government than do even the most debt-ridden farmers.[42] It should not surprise us to learn that, in their search for education, employment, housing, security, and dignity, Negroes of the urban North are more active participants in politics than are other men at a comparable economic or educational level. There is some evidence for the observation that "Negro voting in the low-income brackets runs at a rate double that of whites." [43] Nor should it really surprise us to learn that something near to 4 out of 5 vote Democratic. The Democrats are the party of the poor, the disinherited, and the city streets, and most Negroes are poor and disinherited persons who live on city streets. It would, however, surprise many people who died a generation or more ago. The traditional allegiance of the voting Negro, in the North and South, was to the party of Lincoln. "The Republican party is the ship," Frederick Douglass proclaimed in words that have been quoted a million times. "All else is the sea." Franklin Roosevelt, his colleagues in ethnic politics, and his bounty changed all that in the 1930's. No result of the Roosevelt Revolution was more startling—and yet, like many of its results, quite overdue—than the shift of Negroes from the Republicans to the Democrats. This shift, which resisted even the attraction of Eisenhower, shows few signs of being reversed in the near future. For both racial and economic reasons Negroes in the North are likely to remain down-the-line Democrats. Since there are estimated to be more than four million Negroes of voting age outside the South, this is plainly a fact for the Democrats to cherish—and not to take too much for granted.

Negroes in the South are hardly less faithful Democrats. While the white South split 50-50 between Stevenson and Eisenhower, the Negro South kept the region more solid than it might have been by splitting 60-40 for Stevenson. The Democratic party may be the party of white supremacy, but it is also apparently the party of Negro aspiration. That logic-defying fact may be hard for almost everyone to swallow, from the impartial foreign observer to the partial Southern militant, but the fact exists for all to see. Negro voters in the South, who now total some one million registrants out of a potential of nearly six million,[44] are at one with Negro voters in the North in identifying the Democratic party as the better bet—better but by no means sure—in the struggle for civil rights and economic opportunity.

Religion in politics is a subject of excessive delicacy; one who talks about it at all is sure to be misunderstood if not mistrusted, to raise doubts if not to give offense. Still, there is no use blinking the fact that religion has always played a conspicuous part in determining the political allegiance of Americans. Millions of persons have moved naturally into one or the other party because so many men of their faith were already there. Other millions have shunned one or the other because it appeared to be infested and even controlled by men of a religion they could not abide. And certainly some of the strongest tides of third-party politics have been raised by religious zeal or prejudice.

To descend from abstract history to the concrete present, one may say first of all that, except in a few fossilized pockets of prejudice, religion is no longer an obdurate bar to Americans wishing to switch allegiance from one party to the other. Millions still find it easier to vote for candidates of their own religion, and hundreds of thousands—who knows how many? —find it impossible to vote for candidates of another religion; but both parties now appear as respectable, tolerant havens for men of all faiths. The past, to be sure, dies hard. Although religion is a less powerful influence than it was, let us say, in the

1840's or 1920's, it continues to have a visible if only roughly measurable effect. The assumptions and prejudices we have inherited continue to work in a muffled, furtive way. The pattern of the past was, of course, that outside the South the Democrats were a predominantly Roman Catholic (because predominantly immigrant) party, and that almost everywhere the Republicans were a predominantly Protestant (because predominantly old-stock) party. Even in the most biased and fearful times there were many Catholic Republicans and even more Protestant Democrats, but in many states and cities the cleavage between Democrats and Republicans was at bottom the old cleavage between Catholicism and Protestantism or, to be entirely honest, between Catholicism and anti-Catholicism. The influence of this cleavage has been documented many times over in stories of Catholic industrialists who felt ill at ease among Protestant Republicans, of distressed Scandinavian farmers who could not make the transit from the Republicans to the Democrats and dropped off at the way station of third-party politics, of old ladies who were thrilled by Grover Cleveland or Woodrow Wilson but could not bring themselves to vote "the Romanist ticket."

The pattern of the past persists and, although fainter in outline, shows few signs of disappearing. The Democratic party remains more Catholic than Protestant in style and personnel, the Republican party more Protestant than Catholic in memory and appeal. It is not an accident that the Democrats have furnished the theater in which the drama entitled "A Catholic in the White House?" has settled down for a long run. The Republicans, it is safe to say, are many years away from booking this play into their own theater. (They may, ironically, be the first party to have a Catholic President in the White House, but he will have to come in through the back door of the Vice-Presidency.) And we are many years away from a political system in which religion has nothing to do with the choice of a party. All other things being equal, a Roman Catholic is still more likely to choose to be a Democrat, a Protestant more likely to choose to be a Republican.

To this review of the great historic influences on political behavior and allegiance of Americans—section, locale, class, calling, ethnology, and religion—we should add a few words on three other influences that appear to work more subtly but no less effectively upon us all: age, education, and sex. I have already called attention to the effect of these influences on political activity by observing that middle-aged people are more active than young people, educated people than uneducated, and men than women. The interesting point for us to consider is that, in terms of *age* and *education*, allegiance to Republicanism appears to blossom side-by-side with activity as we move up the scale. Every test of the electorate that has been run in recent years shows that the older or more educated a person is, the more likely he is to vote Republican (and the more likely he is to vote at all); the younger or less educated he is, the more likely he is to vote Democratic (and the less likely he is to vote at all).

Just why this double-barreled fact should be true is not entirely clear. A stronger allegiance to the Democrats among young people is explained partly but not entirely by the suspicions of Republican economics that the new generation has imbibed. A stronger allegiance to the Republicans among well-educated people is explained partly but not entirely by the fact that education and well-being tend to go hand-in-hand. The fact, in any case, is well established, and I think it can be established beyond a doubt in the statistics in Table 9. (These percentages, thanks to the Eisenhower appeal, are clearly more favorable to the Republicans than a table based on congressional elections would be.)

One important qualifying footnote should be appended to the generalization that the farther Americans go with their education, the more likely they are to be Republicans. This

Table 9. Votes and Preferences in the 1952 Presidential Election [45]

	Percentage of population voting for			Total percentage voting	Preference percentages of nonvoters			Total percentage not voting
	Rep.	Dem.	Other		Rep.	Dem.	Other	
Age								
21-34	37	31	—	68	13	17	2	32
35-44	41	34	1	76	11	11	2	24
45-54	45	33	1	79	10	9	2	21
55 and over	48	27	2	77	9	11	3	23
Education								
Grade school	31	30	1	62	15	18	5	38
High school	46	34	—	80	9	10	1	20
College	65	24	1	90	6	4	—	10

may be true of persons who have had postgraduate education for professions like law, medicine, and engineering; it is certainly not true of persons with higher degrees in the sciences, humanities, and social studies. Such people, most of whom are professors, are strongly Democratic in political preference. A careful sample of some 2,400 social scientists engaged in college teaching in 1955 revealed an overwhelming 2 to 1 majority for the Democrats,[46] this despite the fact that the background and status of this group should have led it to a 2 to 1 preference for the Republicans. Even a casual survey of departments of English, history, sociology, physics, or mathematics at almost any college in the country would reveal a similar pattern, and the anti-Republican urge would be even stronger among painters, poets, dramatists, musicians, entertainers, and others engaged in esthetic or intellectual pursuits. The journals of America may be owned by Republicans, but they are largely written by Democrats. (In the light of the overwhelming support given by the newspapers of the country to Eisenhower, it is obviously more important to own than to write.) The "egghead vote" in

America is not a large one, but for what it is worth it is heavily Democratic. It does not go in much for organization; it likes to maintain an air of independence. Yet when the time approaches to go to the polls, most intellectuals come down hard on the side of the field where the memory of Franklin D. Roosevelt is still fresh and appealing. That memory, strengthened by the mutual antipathy of professors and businessmen, will keep them voting Democratic for years to come.

Sex is not quite so obvious or decisive a factor as is age or education in determining long-range allegiance, yet it does count in a small way. What evidence we have suggests two things: that women are becoming more active and independent (of their husbands, that is) as the years since 1919 pass by, and that they are slightly, but only slightly, more willing to vote Republican than men, apparently out of a sharper fear of inflationary prices. Sex can be more of a factor in triggering the occasional switch in which Americans like to indulge. Women appear to be more easily moved than men by candidates of the other party who generate unusual "sex appeal," whatever that is. So long as more candidates are men than women, so long, I suppose, will women appear more politically fickle.[47]

When all these elements of American political demography have been reported and weighed, one that I have not even mentioned will still loom up as the most important single determinant of all, and that, of course, is *inheritance*, which in its turn is the vehicle for the kind of traditionalism that maintains "little enclaves of Democrats in New Hampshire who trace their political ancestry back" to a love for Andrew Jackson and little enclaves of Republicans in Alabama who trace theirs back to a dislike of Jefferson Davis.[48] The family example and the family tie are as powerful forces in our politics as they are in all our social doings. Some persons rebel against their families, but most do not, whether in matters of taste or religion or prejudice or politics. Most Americans—the generally accepted figure is 75 per cent—vote the way their parents voted.[49]

They may maintain the ancestral allegiance, of course, because they occupy the same level of status or income as their parents, or because they are of the same religion or calling. Yet they may also maintain it because they drank it in with the other early influences of their home environment. Habit is a more common influence than emotional rebellion or rational choice in determining social behavior, and many more persons than not go comfortably through life with the politics that held sway in those breeding grounds of habit, the homes in which they were raised. Birthright Republicans and birthright Democrats provide a large majority of the contestants and spectators in the American political arena.

I end this survey of the demography of American politics as I began it—by warning of the pitfalls that are strewn all along this line of approach. It is illusory to think of the electorate as a collection of inert blocs shaped by blind forces, difficult to isolate and measure the influence of any one force out of the many that shape the politics of any one person, gratuitous to ignore the large part that rational choice and deep-seated prejudice play in determining both the long-range preferences and short-range choices of millions of Americans.[50]

Still, if we mind our step and are alert to the pitfalls, we can make excellent use of the broad generalizations that the Democrats are a party of the South, the city, the poor, the unions, the hard-luck farmers, the immigrants and their children, Negroes, white supremacists, the young, the least educated, and the most educated; the Republicans a party of the North, the country, suburbia, the rich, the middle class, the business community, the good-luck farmers, the old stock, the middle-aged, and the college graduates. In making these generalizations, we must note that we are speaking of tendencies more than of imperatives. Both parties can still claim to be all things to all men.

Above all, we must be careful to pay homage to American individualism. As we travel over the political landscape we may come across the perfect demographic Democrat—a poor, young, unionized, Roman Catholic, second-generation, un-skilled laborer named Grabowski with an eighth-grade education and a lumpy bed in Buffalo—and find that he votes the straight Republican ticket, or the perfect demographic Republican—a well-to-do, middle-aged, salaried, Protestant, seventh-genera-tion, top-management executive named Hoover with a college degree and a lovely home in Scarsdale—and find that he votes Democratic and, in addition, throws in $500 a year. The Republicans will be happy to have Grabowski's vote, the Democrats will invite Hoover to sit at the head table at the Jefferson-Jackson day dinner, and political demographers will be reminded once again of the hazards of their trade. Al-though millions of Americans find it impossible to break out of the demographic mold, other millions are sociologically and psychologically free to swear allegiance to either or neither party. Plainly this is a good thing for American democracy.

IV

Democrats or Republicans:
What Difference Does It Make?

ON a crisp evening in September 1959 I had the pleasant experience of lecturing on recent trends in American political thought to an audience at the University of Stellenbosch in South Africa. For an hour or more, while my listeners followed the exposition attentively in a display of true, old-world courtesy, I spun out the story of the intellectual reaction in recent years against the unbuttoned optimism of the Jeffersonian tradition. My speech made pointed reference to the writings of Lippmann, Niebuhr, Riesman, Fromm, Mills, Buckley, Schlesinger, Morgenthau, and Kirk, but almost no reference to current issues and none at all to party politics. It was, indeed, the nearest thing to a purely nonpolitical speech one could make about the United States of America. Yet when it was over, the first question from the floor was: "Would you tell us, sir, what the difference is between a Republican and a Democrat?"

The question did not surprise me in the least. It had been put to me in one form or another at the end of every lecture I had given in that country, no matter what the subject. It had been put to me a thousand times in my own country. There is no doubt that it is a perplexing and fascinating question, and I recognize my clear duty to answer it in all the fine and loving detail it deserves. My answer, I fear, will prove unsatisfactory to many, because in some important respects there is and can be no real difference between the Democrats and the Republicans, because the unwritten laws of American politics demand that the parties overlap substantially in principle, policy, character, appeal, and purpose—or cease to be parties with any hope of winning a national election. Yet if there are necessary similarities between the Democrats and the Republicans, there are also necessary differences, and we must have them clearly in mind before we can say that we understand the politics of American democracy.*

---

* The classic statement of the point of view that there is no real difference between the parties was made by Bryce in *The American Commonwealth:*

There are now two great and several minor parties in the United States. The great parties are the Republicans and the Democrats. What are their principles, their distinctive tenets, their tendencies? Which of them is for free trade, for civil service reform, for a spirited foreign policy, for the regulation of telegraphs by legislation, for a national bankrupt law, for changes in the currency, for any other of the twenty issues which one hears discussed in the country as seriously involving its welfare?

This is what a European is always asking of intelligent Republicans and intelligent Democrats. He is always asking because he never gets an answer. The replies leave him in deeper perplexity. After some months the truth begins to dawn upon him. Neither party has anything definite to say on these issues; neither party has any principles, any distinctive tenets. Both have traditions. Both claim to have tendencies. Both have certainly war cries, organizations, interests enlisted in their support. But those interests are in the main the interests of getting or keeping the patronage of the government. Tenets and policies, points of political doctrine and points of political practice, have all but vanished. They have not been thrown away but have been stripped away by Time and the progress of events, fulfilling some policies, blotting out others. All has been lost, except office or the hope of it.[1]

The parties themselves—the leaders, organizers, propagandists, and "card carriers" of our two enduring coalitions—seem to have a number of differences clearly in their minds, or should I say firmly in their viscera? Emotion, after all, is a vital ingredient of politics, and our parties are about as divided on emotional grounds as we would want them to be. Scratch a real Republican and you will find a man with a deep suspicion of the Democrats. Scratch a real Democrat and you will find a man at least as ready to assault the Republicans as he is to bicker with his own colleagues. Perhaps the best way to measure the emotional gap between the two parties is to talk in terms of images. What image does each party have of itself? What image does it have of the other party? These are admittedly vague questions to which one can give only vague answers that are derived largely from a process best described as "intuitive empiricism." Yet the questions are important; they deal with some of the essential considerations of party allegiance and party division in this country. We must answer them as best we can.

Certainly the Democrats have a fairly clear self-image of themselves, and one need not read far at all in their platforms, speeches, and appeals to learn that the image is, altogether naturally, colorful and flattering. Those Democrats who raise their eyes occasionally above the consuming, two-act spectacle of the struggle for victory and the divison of its spoils make much, perhaps too much, of their fabulous past. They celebrate the achievements of the party, paying special attention to its domestic and diplomatic leadership in the twentieth century and, in addition, insisting that it is pre-eminently "the party of the most liberty and opportunity for the most people." They salute its heroes, of whom four—Jefferson, Jackson, Wilson, and Roosevelt—loom over the landscape of memory like giants, which they were. They delight in the whole sweep of American history, certain that they have been the "movers and shakers" and their opponents, whether Federalists or Whigs or Republicans, the "stick-in-the-muds." Sometimes their enthusiasm gets the better of their sense of proportion, as when they, having laid claim to Jefferson, lay claim to the Declaration of Independence; but for the most part they have spun their self-congratulatory myths out of the substance of fact—spun nylon out of coal, as it were.

The Democrats, being primarily a party and only incidentally a lodge, are really much more concerned with the present and future than with the past. It is the image of themselves they project into the American future that moves them to their best efforts. They pride themselves as "the party of progress," as the men most willing to experiment boldly with new methods for achieving welfare, security, and prosperity. They pride themselves as "the party of the people," as the men most concerned to scatter the fruits of progress widely among all ranks and classes. They are beginning to pride themselves as "the party of the world," as the men best fitted to carry forward the work of Wilson, Roosevelt, and Truman and to negotiate benevolently and prudently with men of all nations. And deep down inside, where feelings are cherished but not openly flaunted, they pride themselves as "the party of the professionals." They are the men who have brought order to politics; they are the men who have taught the nation its lessons in meaningful compromise. Amateurism is all very well in its place, which is on the fringes of the Democratic party or at the core of the Republican party; but professionalism, be it the professionalism of Southern county bosses or Northern precinct bosses, is the essence of the kind of politics that most Democrats like to practice. The Democrats, in their own opinion, are the "old pros" of American politics. What baseball is for Warren Spahn, basketball for Bob Pettit, and football for Charley Conerly, politics is for them—a vocation that grants its richest rewards to the man who pursues it with dedication, skill, confidence, and a quiet sense of the possible. For every loyal party worker who thinks fondly of Franklin Roosevelt as the Model

Democrat, at least two others think no less fondly of Jim Farley.

To the Republicans this self-molded image of achievement, heroism, liberty, progress, democracy, worldliness, and professional competence appears as a caricature of reality. Even when we make allowance for the natural mistrust of one band of politicians for the other band across the street, we are struck by the intensity of the Republican image of Democratic weakness, wickedness, and false counsel. Republicans usually begin their assessment of the Democratic party by throwing out everything that took place before the Civil War. Jackson is only a name out of a misty past; Jefferson would be happier with the Republicans today than with the Democrats. Whatever services the Democrats performed before the Republicans came upon the scene in 1856, their record ever since has been one of which modern Democrats, if they would ever look up from the anxious toil of keeping a brawling family from breaking up completely, would hardly choose to boast.

The plain fact is that the Republicans, for all the friendly contacts they keep with their counterparts in the Democratic party, look upon that party as a vehicle of demagoguery, radicalism, plunder, socialism, unsound economics, bossism, corruption, subversion, and ill repute. Even the stanchest Republican will boast that some of his "best friends" are Democrats, but even the mildest finds something off-color in the party as a whole. There have been too many patrician demagogues like Roosevelt and too many vulgar ones like Huey Long, too many addlepated "pinks" like Henry Wallace and dangerous ones like R. G. Tugwell, too many big spenders like Harry Truman and big lenders like Dean Acheson and big plunderers like Frank Hague. It is a party much too willing to hazard inflation in the interest of false prosperity and real votes. It is a party racked since time out of mind by big and little bosses who have no principles save that of victory and no interest in victory save that of the spoils. The morals of party politics are never exactly dainty, the Republicans admit, but the morals of Democratic politics are downright shoddy.

Worse than all this, it is a party that cannot be trusted to maintain a patriotic front against the assaults of the nation's acknowledged enemies and the blandishments of its self-styled friends. It has harbored a shocking number of heretics, subversives, and traitors; it has surrendered our freedom of maneuver to the leaders of a dozen other countries, some of them not even friendly; it has squandered American lives and treasure in a vain search for peace and world order. As it was the party of Clement Vallandigham in the 1860's, it was the party of Alger Hiss in the 1940's. "Not all Democrats were rebels," Republican orators shouted as they "waved the bloody shirt" after the Civil War, "but all rebels were Democrats." "Not all Democrats were pinks and subversives," I heard a Republican remark just the other day, "but all pinks and subversives were Democrats—and they still are."

And as it was the party of the Boston Irish in the 1850's, it is the party of the New York Puerto Ricans in the 1960's. This is the last and most repelling element in the total image of the Democratic party held by many good Republicans: it speaks with an accent; it is not quite American; it is just not respectable. And if the accent of the Pole or the Jew or the Puerto Rican is music to the friendly ears of other, perhaps more broad-minded Republicans, there is always the accent of the Southern racist to remind them to stay put in the ranks behind Lincoln and McKinley.

This is, admittedly, a harsh image, not all of whose harshness can be explained as a simple, corrective reaction to the pretensions of the Democrats themselves. It is not an image, fortunately, on which many Republicans dwell obsessively or most Republicans are prepared to act. In the real world of politics, lawmaking, and administration it presents no insurmountable barrier to the bipartisan jockeying and co-operation that makes our system livable and workable. The image is there, nonetheless, carried sturdily in millions of Republican bosoms, and it is perhaps a more important force in the total pattern of our politics than the positive image carried by the Democrats themselves. The latter does not forbid loyal Democrats to go off the reservation; the former makes it an act of heresy for loyal Republicans to embrace the sweaty Democrats.

Let that be the essential image of the Democratic party in which both Democrats and Republicans put stock. It is indeed a sweaty army—heavy with the sweet sweat of toil for the American people, according to the Democrats themselves; reeking with the sour sweat of corruption and "80 per cent Americanism," according to the Republicans.

Democrats will say angrily that, in my review of the achievements and failures of the Republicans in Chapter III, I was much too kind to the Grand Old Party. Republicans will say even more angrily that I was much too cruel. They, too, carry a flattering self-image in their minds, which, because of their fewer years and less motley composition, is a good deal sharper than the self-image of the Democrats. They, too, celebrate their historic achievements, painting them in far brighter colors than the scholarly pastels I have used. Consider these claims in the *Republican Fact-Book* of 1948:

The Republican Party has a long and honorable history of majority control of this country during the most expansive period of its development. Between 1861 and 1933, Republican Presidents were in office three-fourths of the time. They shaped governmental policy which encouraged the development of the country's vast resources; built up its defenses; created its national banking system; established a currency which circulated throughout the world on a par with gold; made the credit of the country the most stable in the world; formulated economic policies which made this country the leader among all nations in agriculture, mining, and manufacturing —in short, made the United States first among the nations.

Having broken the slave bonds of the Negro and made him a free man; having bound up the deep wounds of a nation divided against itself; the Republican Party continued to proceed on a program of adherence to the principles of Constitutional Government which the genius of the founding fathers had laid down. Within the framework of justice and law, the Republican Party built up the confidence of the people in the American Way of Life.[2]

They, too, salute their heroes joyfully. If the Democrats have four giants, they have one, Abraham Lincoln, who is more than a match all by himself for these four and all others the opposition can muster. Lincoln belongs to all Americans, indeed to all men of good will everywhere in the world, but he belongs first of all to the Republicans. He is an essential myth without whom no Republican orator or organizer or platform writer would know just how to proceed. It is possible that Dwight D. Eisenhower is a similar myth in the making.

The *Fact-Book* makes this short, happy statement of "Republican Principles," and catches almost perfectly the feeling millions of Republicans have about their party:

The Republican Party was originated in 1854 as the political group dedicated to the freedom of the individual and the safeguard of his inalienable rights. It has since remained steadfastly devoted to these basic American principles—free initiative, free enterprise, and the dignity of the average man. More than ever the deep significance of the Republican stand for Constitutionalism, States' Rights, encouragement of American enterprise and a minimum of Government interference with freedom of opportunity becomes apparent today when the extent to which these principles have been whittled down by the Democrat Party is realized.

Here is the essence of true Republicanism, even in these days of the modern, domesticated, politely New Dealish party: individualism as opposed to collectivism, free enterprise as opposed to "socialistic meddling," constitutionalism as opposed to "one-man rule," states' rights as opposed to centralization. It is, indeed, the party of "the American Way of Life." It took the lead in building the Way; it has defended it patriotically against subversion and radicalism; it is, in a real sense, the Way Incarnate. I do not mean this at all facetiously when I say that the average Republican is much readier than the average Demo-

crat to identify his own party with the nation and its household
gods—home, mother, the flag, and free enterprise.

A final ingredient in the Republican self-image is the warm feeling of respectability that characterizes the record, principles, operations, and tone of the party. It is businesslike without being coldly professional, sound without being callous, steady without being stale. It is "100 per cent American," not only in the stout fight it puts up for American principles, but in the mood in which it thinks, the temper in which it acts, the accent in which it speaks. Here, in particular, the image the Republicans have of themselves needs the image they have of the Democrats to bring it into sharp focus. The Democrats are plainly a disreputable crowd; the Republicans, by contrast, are men of standing and sobriety. Many a middle-class American in many a small town has had to explain painfully why he chose to be a Democrat. No middle-class American need feel uneasy as a Republican. Even when he is a minority—for example, among the heathen on a college campus—he can, like any white, Anglo-Saxon Protestant, warm himself before his little fire of self-esteem.*

The Democrats find all this talk of the American Way of Life

---

* The situation described by Brand Whitlock in the Ohio of his youth still exists in many parts of America:

In such an atmosphere as that in the Ohio of those days it was natural to be a Republican; it was more than that, it was inevitable that one should be a Republican; it was not a matter of intellectual choice, it was a process of biological selection. The Republican party was not a faction, not a group, not a wing, it was an institution like those Emerson speaks of in his essay on Politics, rooted like oak trees in the center around which men group themselves as best they can. It was a fundamental and self-evident thing, like life, and liberty, and the pursuit of happiness, or like the flag or the federal judiciary. It was elemental like gravity, the sun, the stars, the ocean. It was merely a synonym for patriotism, another name for the nation. One became, in Urbana and in Ohio for many years, a Republican just as the Eskimo dons fur clothes. It was inconceivable that any self-respecting man should be a Democrat. There were, perhaps, Democrats in Lighttown; but then there were rebels in Alabama, and in the Ku Klux Klan, about which we read in the evening, in the Cincinnati *Gazette*.[3]

a sham and a bore. The Republican party with which they have
to contend is a pompous, superpatriotic, self-centered, hypo-
critical band of hard-minded men with a unique penchant for
serving themselves while insisting that they are serving all
America. Who are they, ask the Democrats, to shout about individualism when they fought so bitterly against all attempts
to rescue helpless individuals in the 1930's? Who are they to
wave the bloody shirt of treason against the administrations of
Roosevelt and Truman when they yapped and snarled at almost
every constructive step toward leadership of the free world?
Who are they to shout the glories of free enterprise when they
have always banked so heavily on the government for friendly
support of their schemes? Who are they to strike a posture of
purity and wag their finger at the corruption of the city machines when they took favors from this government—protective
tariffs, subsidies, land grants—that were worth billions rather
than millions? The Republicans may rejoice in the memory of
Lincoln, but if Lincoln were here today he would have a hard
time warming to a single man in Eisenhower's Cabinet.

The essence of the Democratic image of the Republican
party is the certain knowledge that, for all its protestations
about liberty and justice for every American, it is the party of
the few, of the rich, of the interests, of the upper classes. It is
constitutionally incapable of looking out over the whole of
America and, in the skillful, purposeful manner of the Democrats, of caring for the legitimate needs of all ranks and callings.
It takes no broad view; it thinks no big thoughts; it has no
warm heart. It is not creative in domestic affairs, for the best
it has been able to do throughout a generation of Democratic
innovation and progress is first to shout "Good God! No!" and
then "Me, too!" It is not reliable in foreign affairs, for it has
repeatedly confused our friends and neighbors with its threats
and boasts and changes of mind. It is not even what a conservative party is supposed to be: sound and prudent and steady.
The Republicans, not the Democrats, produced the wildest

demagogue in American history and backed him with zeal. The Republican party is indeed a minority, the Democrats conclude, in the range of its interests as well as in numbers. It is a minority, that is to say, because it deserves to be a minority.

If we can discount the natural excesses of admiration and abuse that are present in these pairs of images, we can come up with some fairly useful generalizations about the character of our two parties. To speak of the character of a group of human beings as numerous and formless as an American party is an exercise in illusion, for it is to personalize the impersonal and individualize the collective. Yet one cannot spend much time in the clubhouses and convention halls in which the parties do their political business without becoming aware of certain vague but substantial differences in character or, as I prefer, style. A gathering of Democrats *is* more sweaty, disorderly, offhand, and rowdy than a gathering of Republicans; it is also likely to be more cheerful, imaginative, tolerant of dissent, and skillful at the game of give-and-take. A gathering of Republicans *is* more respectable, sober, purposeful, and businesslike than a gathering of Democrats; it is also likely to be more self-righteous, pompous, cut-and-dried, and just plain boring. In a Republican office one hears much talk of programs and policies; at a Republican convention the color and excitement, such as they are, seem labored and staged. In a Democratic clubhouse one hears much talk of votes and voters; at a Democratic convention the color and excitement are generated by the delegates themselves. Republicans seem to lean to the ideological side of politics, Democrats to the practical. The most famous of all "smoke-filled rooms" (Colonel Harvey's at the Blackstone in Chicago in 1920) was, to be sure, inhabited by Republicans, but I have the distinct impression—distinct as only the impressions of a nonsmoker can be—that the air is bluer and thicker and yet somehow softer in any room where Democrats have gathered to do their immemorial business.

Taken all-in-all, the two parties show two of the familiar

faces of America, much alike in respects that would catch the attention of the foreign observer, somewhat different in those for which an American with a sharp sociological eye would be looking. A writer who has been, in his time, to many political conventions and to even more business luncheons once summed it up for me by remarking, "The Republicans look to me like Rotarians at the speakers' table, the Democrats like Rotarians at table 16, back near the entrance to the kitchen." Those at the speakers' table, we agreed, are just a little bit stiff, correct, falsely hearty, and conscious of their eminence. No angry voice is raised to mar their unity of principle and purpose. They all wear vests, they all smile brightly, they all sing the familiar songs with fervor. They are leaders of the community, and they know it. Meanwhile, back at table 16, things are more relaxed and less self-conscious. Arguments are aired with abandon and settled (or forgotten) with a shrug. Dress is more casual, salutes are more boisterous, jokes are more earthy. They may be leaders, too, but at the moment they are just the boys at table 16. The respectable Republicans who delight in their polite unity, the relaxed Democrats who cherish their rowdy variety—they are all good Americans together, but there is a difference in their styles. That difference is caught vividly in the choice of beastly emblems that was made for all of us long ago: the slightly ridiculous but tough and long-lived Donkey —the perfect symbol of the rowdy Democrats; the majestic but ponderous Elephant—the perfect symbol of the respectable Republicans. Can anyone imagine the Donkey as a Republican or the Elephant as a Democrat?

The last few pages have been fun for my readers, I hope, but they take us only a little way toward a confident grasp of the real differences between the two parties, by which I mean differences in principle and program rather than in style or behavior, differences that can be observed and then acted upon rationally by Americans who must go to the polls and choose between candidates of the two parties, differences that our friends abroad can expect to feel with the change-over from a Democratic to a Republican Congress or a Republican to a Democratic President. Americans who ask plaintively about these differences are really asking if their votes are likely to have any effect beyond throwing one set of rascals out and another set in. Without regard to the personal merits of the candidates or the cut-and-thrust of the issues in any particular election, is there a meaningful distinction, they wonder, between the act of voting Democratic and the act of voting Republican? Does it matter at all whether a Democrat or Republican sits in the governor's chair in Connecticut or serves as senior senator from Illinois or represents the third congressional district of Oregon? Does it make any difference which party controls the House of Representatives, has a majority in the Federal Trade Commission, and, above all, owns the White House?

The short answer to these persistent questions is that it matters somewhat more than most people realize and somewhat less than most people seem to want it to matter. I base this answer on four major considerations: the large achievements and failures we noted in Chapter III; the voting record of each party on the key issues of the half-century between the going of Cleveland and the coming of Franklin Roosevelt; the voting record in the years of the New Deal, World War II, and the Fair Deal; and the virility of each party's present and probable future commitment to the new responsibilities of government that grew out of the New Deal and have been perpetuated in the welfare-warfare state.

We can make short work of the first of these considerations by looking back a fair but not ridiculous distance—let us say, to 1876—and by summing up the differences between the two parties as makers of history in this generalization. The Republicans had a good deal more than the Democrats to do with the glories and trials of the Age of Enterprise, the five or more decades in which America moved under the guidance of the Rockefellers, Carnegies, and Fords, not to mention James G. Blaine, William McKinley, Mark Hanna, Nelson Aldrich, and Theodore Roosevelt, into the now familiar position of the world's leading industrial power. To the extent that this country can ever be said to have been directed or shaped by merely political activity, the America of 1900 or 1925—strong, secure, expansive, dynamic, bountiful, and yet somehow troubled— was essentially their creation. The Democrats played their part, too, but it was a reluctant, awkward, secondary part in a great drama in which the Republicans had set the stage and continued to dominate it.

Conversely, the Democrats had a good deal more than the Republicans to do with the glories and trials of the Age of Roosevelt, the two or more decades in which America moved under the guidance of Franklin Roosevelt, his colleagues, and his heirs into the complexities of the New Economy at home and the New Internationalism abroad. The America of 1950—strong, secure, expansive, dynamic, bountiful, and in addition more just and humane, and in further addition more troubled—was essentially their creation. The Republicans played their part, too, but like the Democrats of 1900 they were not, certainly as a party, in the front ranks of the procession into the future. It is up to each American to decide which America he would prefer to live in—not that he really has any choice but to live in the second—and thus to give the nod of history to the one party or the other. The abstract choice, in any case, should not be impossible to make, for, despite their many common services and disservices to the American people, each of the parties has made its own distinctive contribution to the rise and splendor of the United States.

Did it make any difference over the long course of history whether one voted Republican or Democrat? Surely it did.

We can make short work of the second consideration, too, by noting that in the years between 1896 and 1932 the Democrats, even with Alton B. Parker and John W. Davis as their standard bearers, never lost the Bryan touch and never ceased to disturb the business community, while the Republicans, even with Theodore Roosevelt in the White House or George Norris in the Senate, never lost the McKinley touch and almost never failed the business community when the going was rough. Both parties, as always, shilly-shallied grotesquely on some of the hottest issues of the time. Both, as always, were reluctant to take clear-cut stands in defiance of any articulate group in the American electorate. Yet a quick review of the roll calls in Congress during these years, bolstered by a quick comparison of the ideas and actions of Woodrow Wilson with those of the Republican President at either end of his incumbency, proves that the Democrats were even then a more reform-minded party than were the Republicans. Men of progressive bent could not look to either party for a concerted plan of attack on the problems of our industrial infancy, but the Democrats were almost always a trifle readier to regulate business in behalf of the less fortunate members of society—with the aid of insurgent Western Republicans who should have been Democrats but could not leap over the old walls of sectionalism, ethnology, and memory.

The real issue on which the parties divided in those days was, of course, the tariff. Voters throughout the country and interested observers abroad were well aware that a Republican Congress meant a higher protective tariff, a Democratic Congress an attempt to bring it lower. Both Cleveland and Wilson were pledged unequivocally to a reduction in the tariff, and both did their best to make good on their pledges. The great struggles over the tariff between 1888 and 1932 were, as much as such struggles ever can be in our fuzzy-edged system, party struggles. In several of the most desperate of these—for example, the maneuvers and votes over the McKinley Act of 1890, the Wilson Act of 1894, and the Underwood Act of 1913—the mavericks in the ranks of each party were few indeed. No one had to ask what was the difference between the Republicans and Democrats in the seven mighty struggles over the tariff between 1888 and 1932.[4] The Democrats, with only a handful of dissenters sidetracked by sectional interests, went down the line for reduction; the Republicans, on some occasions without a single dissenter, went down the line for a higher and ever higher tariff. In the last great vote on this question before the coming of Franklin D. Roosevelt—the passage of the modern version of "the Tariff of Abominations," the Smoot-Hawley Act of 1930—the parties split as follows: in the Senate, for the act 39 Republicans and against it 11, for the act 5 Democrats and against it 30; in the House, for the act 208 Republicans and against it 20, for the act 14 Democrats and against it 132. This was, by any American definition, a genuine party vote. To our overstuffed and jaded political minds the question of tariff legislation hardly seems earth-shaking, but in those days of limited government a tariff act was the most powerful influence that Congress could visit on the nation's economy. Here, surely, was a sharp point of disagreement between the two parties.

Did it make any difference whether one voted Republican or Democrat? It did indeed, and the difference counted.

The difference was still there in 1934 when the New Deal, under the leadership of a Democratic President who had pledged himself to tariff reduction, took its first swing at the problem. The Reciprocal Trade Agreements Act, of which Cordell Hull was the immediate father, was passed by a vote that divided the parties in the Senate as follows: for the act 51 Democrats and against it 5; for the act 5 Republicans and against it 28. (There was a voice vote in the House.) This, too, was a party vote, and it was the kind that was to be recorded again and again in the years of Franklin D. Roosevelt and Harry S. Truman—a vote in which most of the Democrats in Congress chose to take some new step into the future that would involve more spending of public funds and more responsibility for government, and in which most of the Republicans (in part, of course, out of a natural urge to thwart Roosevelt and Truman) held back or went along grudgingly. Throughout the two decades of Democratic supremacy, the Democrats were generally a reform party, the Republicans a conservative party—and most Americans seemed to recognize this fact clearly. I have trudged through the important roll calls in Congress from the Agricultural Adjustment Act of 1933 to the Tidelands Oil Act of 1952, and I think that this is a fair observation.[5] It was Democratic votes, Democratic politics, Democratic principles, Democratic Presidents that carried us toward more welfare and regulation at home and toward more adventure and involvement abroad. The Republicans, to the contrary, held out against both these trends as best and as long as they could. Not until after World War II, when the new ways of Franklin Roosevelt had begun to harden into a new set of deeply vested, widely shared interests, did they give up their opposition to the reforms and adventures of the New Deal and start to claim them as their own. Their claims are not worth a great deal in the light of the voting records on these crucial domestic and foreign issues of the "twenty long years" (Table 10).*

* I am aware of the limited value and the dangers of such a table as this. These figures give no indication of the jockeying that went on for weeks before each final vote, nor do they account for the range of enthusiasm or the varieties of motivation that marked the votes of the Fors and the Againsts on each major issue. For example, it cannot be denied that the Republican urge to vote Against on most issues between 1933–1952 was heightened by the desire to vote against Roosevelt and Truman. Still, I have done my best to choose examples of votes in which the conflict between "liberalism" and "conservatism" (or between "internationalism" and "isolationism") was a matter of common knowledge, in which opposition to (or support of) the President was a relatively minor factor in sharpening the division, and in which the final vote was, except where noted, the "crucial vote" on the particular issue. I am not seeking, because no one could find, scientific accuracy in this presentation. I am seeking evidence of tendencies that have separated the two parties in this generation.

Table 10. Voting Records, 1933–1952

Acts or treaties	Party	House vote		Senate vote	
		For	Against	For	Against
Domestic issues					
T.V.A., 1933	Dem.	284	2	48	3
	Rep.	17	89	14	17
	Other	5	—	1	—
N.R.A., 1933	Dem.	266	25	46	4
	Rep.	53	50	10	20
	Other	4	—	1	—
A.A.A., 1933	Dem.	272	24	48	5
	Rep.	39	73	14	15
	Other	4	1	1	—
Public Utilities, 1934	Dem.	203	59		
	Rep.	7	83	Voice vote	
	Other	9	0		
Social Security, 1935	Dem.	287	13	60	1
	Rep.	77	18	14	5
	Other	7	2	2	—
Rider to return control of relief to states, 1936	Dem.			1	50
	Rep.	Not before House		13	4
	Other				3
Soil Conservation, 1936	Dem.	246	25	49	9
	Rep.	20	64	5	11
	Other	1	8	2	—
Housing, 1937	Dem.	239	38	55	8
	Rep.	24	48	6	8
	Other	12	—	3	—
Wages and Hours, 1938	Dem.	247	41		
	Rep.	31	48	Voice vote	
	Other	12	—		
A.A.A., 1938	Dem.	243	54	53	17
	Rep.	14	74	2	11
	Other	6	7	1	3
School Lunch Program, 1946	Dem.	164	45	38	4
	Rep.	110	56	11	17
				(crucial vote)	

Table 10. Voting Records, 1933–1952 (*continued*)

Acts or treaties	Party	House vote		Senate vote	
		For	Against	For	Against
Taft-Hartley, 1947	Dem.	103	66	17	15
	Rep.	217	12	37	2
	Other	—	1	—	—
Portal-to-Portal Pay, 1947	Dem.	116	50	18	22
(unfavorable to labor)	Rep.	229	5	46	2
Rent Control, 1949	Dem.	199	52	48	2
	Rep.	61	101	5	31
				(crucial vote)	
Public Health, 1951	Dem.	Did not act		28	10
	Rep.			10	25
Tidelands Oil, 1952	Dem.	94	70	24	24
	Rep.	153	18	26	11

Foreign issues

World Court, 1935	Dem.	No vote required		43	20
	Rep.			9	14
	Other			—	2
Selective Service, 1940	Dem.	211	33	50	17
	Rep.	52	112	8	10
	Other	—	14	—	4
Lend-Lease, 1941	Dem.	236	25	49	13
	Rep.	24	135	10	17
	Other	—	5	1	1
Selective Service Extension, 1941	Dem.	182	65	38	16
	Rep.	21	133	7	13
	Other	—	4	—	1
British Loan, 1946	Dem.	157	32	29	15
	Rep.	61	122	17	18
	Other	1	1	—	1
Greece-Turkey Aid, 1947	Dem.	160	13	32	7
	Rep.	127	93	35	16
	Other	—	1	—	—

Table 10. Voting Records, 1933–1952 (*continued*)

Acts or treaties	Party	House vote		Senate vote	
		For	Against	For	Against
Foreign Assistance, 1948	Dem.	150	11		
	Rep.	167	62	Voice vote	
	Other	—	2		
Selective Service, 1948	Dem.	136	31		
	Rep.	123	103	Voice vote	
	Other	—	2		
Military Assistance, 1949	Dem.	172	24		
	Rep.	51	84	Voice vote	
	Other	—	1		
UNRRA, 1949	Dem.	185	9	30	7
	Rep.	149	45	16	7
	Other	4	—	—	—
Trade Agreements Extension, 1949	Dem.	234	6	47	1
	Rep.	84	63	15	18
Yugoslav Emergency Relief, 1950	Dem.	182	41	35	7
	Rep.	43	100	25	14
Mutual Security, 1952	Dem.	168	20	39	1
	Rep.	78	89	25	9

By the late 1940's, as this table shows, the Republicans themselves had been pretty well caught up in the tides of the new times, yet again and again it was from their direction that voices were raised most angrily against some new move toward welfare at home and involvement abroad. When the House voted 351 to 9 on the modest Housing Act of 1948, the nine nay-sayers were all Republicans; when it voted 361 to 22 to liberalize grants and procedures under the Social Security Act in 1952, all but two of the standpatters were Republicans. When the Senate voted 90 to 2 to confirm our entrance into the United Nations, the two recalcitrants were Republicans; when it voted 82 to 13 to accept the North Atlantic Treaty, eleven of the thirteen skeptics were Republicans. The guardians of the old America had dwindled to a small platoon, but students of our politics knew where to find most of them.

Did it make any difference in the 1930's and 1940's whether one voted Republican or Democrat? Surely it did.

Those days are gone, however, and we are living in the 1960's. It is, therefore, the fourth consideration that must weigh most heavily with us. What is the virility of each party's commitment to the new responsibilities of American government? Which is quicker to support more social security at home and more aid to underdeveloped countries abroad? Which is more likely to take the next giant step toward the full welfare state by instituting a scheme of socialized medicine? Which is more likely, in the event of a rough passage for the American economy, to use the powers of subsidy and control the government already holds and to ask for more?

The answer to all these questions is, for better or worse, the Democrats. They got us into our present commitments, and for some time to come they will be more at home with them, which must also mean that they are readier to take on a few more. The Republicans will honor these commitments, in their votes as well as in their programs, but for some time to come they will do it with the air of men who live in "a world they never made," which must also mean that they will not go searching anxiously, in the image of a Wayne Morse or Hubert Humphrey, for more. Consider the votes in Table 11 on important issues to come up during Eisenhower's Presidency.

I do not know how others may interpret these tables, but to me they prove that the Democrats and the Republicans are still at least a city block apart on issues like taxation, welfare, farm subsidies, regulation of business, regulation of labor, the tariff, and "foreign entanglements." The Democrats have held the whip hand for the better part of a generation; and, despite the dissensions in their own team, they have used their superior power and sense of purpose to move us at a pretty fast clip—

Table 11. Voting Records, 1953–1959

Acts or treaties	Party	House vote		Senate vote	
		For	Against	For	Against
Domestic issues					
Tidelands Oil (an act desired by the oil companies), 1953	Dem.	94	70	24	24
	Rep.	153	18	26	11
Agriculture (providing for flexible price supports and thus not wholly acceptable to farm interests), 1954	Dem.			18	24
	Rep.	Voice vote		44	3
	Other			—	1
Tax Reduction, 1954	Dem.	114	73	19	22
	Rep.	201	3	42	3
	Other	—	1	—	1
Amendment to Atomic Energy Act (under which A.E.C. is to favor public bodies and co-operatives in disposing of excess power from its plants), 1954	Dem.			38	6
	Rep.	Voice vote		6	35
	Other			1	—
Public Housing Act, 1955	Dem.	153	37	Voice vote	
	Rep.	35	131		
Harris-Fulbright Bill (exempting natural gas producers from direct federal rate control), 1956	Dem.	86	136	22	24
	Rep.	123	67	31	14
			(vetoed)		
Agricultural Bill (setting up soil bank and restoring high, rigid support prices), 1956	Dem.	189	35	35	4
	Rep.	48	146	15	31
National Defense Education, 1958 (an Eisenhower "must")	Dem.	140	30	37	7
	Rep.	72	55	29	8
T.V.A. Self-Financing (giving T.V.A. power to finance new facilities), 1959	Dem.	238	31	56	2
	Rep.	7	139	17	15
Public Works Appropriation Bill (a notable "spending" measure), 1959	Dem.	266	4	55	1
	Rep.	46	89	18	14
			(vetoed)		

Table 11. Voting Records, 1953–1959 (*continued*)

Acts or treaties	Party	House vote		Senate vote	
		For	Against	For	Against
Labor Reform Act, 1959	Dem.*	95	184	15	44
	Rep.	134	17	32	2
		(vote on amendment to substitute Landrum-Griffin bill for committee bill more favorable to labor)		(Vote on so-called McClellan amendment, bitterly opposed by organized labor)	
Foreign issues					
Foreign Aid, 1953	Dem.	126	29		
	Rep.	94	80	Voice vote	
	Other	1	—		
Refugee immigration (providing only limited entry of refugees), 1953	Dem.	88	111	24	22
	Rep.	132	74	38	8
Mutual Security (providing additional foreign aid), 1954	Dem.	144	43	29	7
	Rep.	121	85	12	26
	Other	—	—	—	1
Reciprocal Trade Extention Act, 1958	Dem.	184	39	40	6
	Rep.	133	59	32	12
Foreign Aid, 1959	Dem.	182	83		
	Rep.	89	59	Voice vote	

* Of the 95 Democratic "antilabor" votes in the House 85 were cast by Southerners; of the 15 such votes in the Senate 11 were cast by Southerners.

The first important vote in the session of 1960—on a bill in the Senate for substantial federal aid to education—found 54 in favor (46 Democrats and 8 Republicans) and 35 opposed (11 Democrats, of whom 10 were Southerners, and 24 Republicans).

fast, in any case, for American tastes—along the road to Big Government with Big Responsibilities. The Republicans have been forced by political considerations, the march of events, and the more progressive members of their own team to aban-

don their original posture of obdurate opposition to this trend
and to follow the Democrats at a safe distance. The Democrats
have been resting for some years now, partly through choice
and partly through circumstance, and the Republicans seem to
have caught up all along the line. They vote dutifully and almost
as enthusiastically as the Democrats for appropriations to keep
the Social Security Administration and our delegation to the
United Nations in business, and they are supported in their
votes by a majority of those in the ranks. A survey of regular
Republican sentiment in 1952 on some of the famous legacies
of Roosevelt and Truman showed these results: [6]

	Good thing	Mistake	Neither good or bad	No opinion
Social Security laws	84%	6%	7%	3%
Farm price supports	39	34	13	14
Tennessee Valley Authority	58	15	10	17
Recognition of labor unions	42	24	11	23
Marshall Plan	47	18	19	16

The Republicans only "seem" to have caught up, however,
and when the next lunge forward at home or abroad is taken
by the Democrats, as it must be taken sooner or later, they
will (and, as conservatives, should) drop back again to the
distance of that safe city block. Let me put the difference in
terms of time rather than space: The Republicans have been
traveling the same road as the Democrats, but they are ten to
fifteen years behind and have not enjoyed the trip nearly so
much. They did not plan to take it in the first place, and besides
they have had to swallow a lot of dust—an occupational hazard
with which men who prefer to be conservatives must learn to
live. In any case it is not surprising that the Republican commitment to social security, aid to farmers, active diplomacy, or
regulation of the air waves is clearly less enthusiastic than that
of the Democrats, the men who got there first under Roosevelt

and Truman. This fact shows up in the administration of all those laws that Roosevelt left behind. Barring the ever-present factor of individual personality and character, it does make a difference to the television industry, the railroads, or the stock exchanges whether Democrats or Republicans have a majority in the independent commissions.

The difference between Democrats and Republicans, which I find to be the conflict of liberalism (currently jaded) and conservatism (always opportunistic), might also be stated in this homespun way: The Democrats are more willing to spend money than the Republicans, and thus more willing to raise taxes. Many Democrats make a fetish of economy in government—the champion economizer, after all, is Senator Harry Byrd—and all profess to be as anxious as the Republicans to "bring relief to the hard-pressed taxpayer," especially in an election year. Many Republicans play the game of logrolling as expertly and lavishly as the most carefree Democrats. Yet the roll calls on money bills in Congress are evidence of somewhat different views in our two parties toward the public treasury. Democrats are, in a word, freer with public funds; Republicans are, in another word, tighter. Conversely, Republicans are more alarmed at the prospect of inflation; Democrats care about it, too, but not all that much. They have many more loyal constituents than do the Republicans among those classes in our society that need a break in the form of unemployment checks, maternity benefits, and low-rent housing. They can therefore be expected to appropriate funds with less concern about where the money is to be found or what its distribution will do to the level of prices. The Republicans, as we know, find their most loyal constituents among those classes that need no break in the form of subsidies, but that would like to hang on to more of what they already have—and have more to hang on to. They can therefore be expected to take up the cudgels, both in season and out, for budget cutting and tax reduction, and they will justify their exertions as "counterthrusts to the insidious pressures of inflation." The sound dollar and the balanced budget are American institutions of impeccable lineage; the Republicans have a clearly warmer feeling about them than do the Democrats, who are usually reduced to answering back with slogans about a "sound rate of growth" and a "balanced America."

Does it make any difference today whether one votes Republican or Democrat? Surely it does—or at least it could!

Alert readers may notice that I have avoided both rhetorical and statistical comment on two major issues of our time—national defense and civil rights—and they will wonder rightly whether our politicians tend to divide along party lines on these issues, too. My own answer, based on study of the votes in Congress as well as on observation of events during the past decade, is that they do not, at least not in any way that permits us at present to expect any more or different action from a Democratic than from a Republican President or Congress. The whole process of forming policies and making decisions in the area of defense is one in which partisanship has long since given way to bipartisan, nonpartisan, expert, and merely bureaucratic considerations, and these in turn are shaped by circumstances over which no man or agency or group in this country seems to have any direct control. While the debate over national defense goes on hotly and without rest, it is not and apparently cannot be a primarily political debate, and it deals principally in details and methods of administration. The nation is too much agreed on over-all policy in this matter, and men with alternatives to propose—such as building up for an attack on Russia or disarming unilaterally—will get no hearing or support from the two parties. Anyone who can make much party-political sense out of the votes in Congress, the recommendations of the Joint Chiefs of Staff, or the budgets and strategies of the last two Presidents has a talent for research or extrapolation that I cannot claim. Partisan sniping at the President and the leadership in Congress goes on constantly; vague patterns of partisan favoritism toward one service or another emerge from time to time in the House or Senate. They vanish, however, as quickly as they appeared, and I think it fair to say that Democrats and Republicans can be counted on indefinitely to support a "respectable posture of defense" in general and all the services in particular.

To these observations I might append two footnotes of which other, perhaps more partisan observers might wish to make something of a fuss. Party differences over national defense could conceivably be wrenched from two differences in principle and concern I have already mentioned. All other things being equal, a Democrat might be likely to vote with lighter heart than a Republican for an expanded military budget; a Republican might worry a little longer over the inflationary implications of his vote. All other things being equal, a Republican might be more willing than a Democrat to withdraw from one of the alliances to which Roosevelt and Truman first committed us; a Democrat might worry a little longer over the turmoil we might leave behind. If these be differences, they are not large enough to get excited about.

The recent history of civil-rights legislation finds the Democrats camped on both sides of the Republicans, who mill about in the middle in more than the usual confusion. The most ardent proponents of strong federal action in this field are Democrats from the Northern cities, where discrimination hurts and something can be done about it, and the most ardent opponents are Democrats from the rural South, where discrimination is a way of life and nothing is going to be done about it if they can help it. One reason for the fact of federal inaction is the hog-tied position of the federal government, and the reason for that, as the world knows, is the obdurate power of the Southern Democrats in the House and Senate. So long as that power exists and no concerted attempt is made to break it, it will be hard for the Democrats to pose as the party of civil rights.

The Republicans are not a great deal happier or more

united in this matter. Their attitudes extend from the aggressive instincts of a Javits to the doughface standpattism of a Mason, not forgetting the seven Republicans who represent the South in the House. The party of Lincoln has special reasons for mounting a strong, persistent attack on discrimination, yet this calls for government action of an aggressive, tradition-shattering nature, something with which Republicans are, in temper and on principle, understandably less comfortable than are Northern Democrats. For the time being, that is, so long as the Republicans are the more conservative of our two parties (which may be forever) and the Democrats a party of both North and South (which may not be forever), there will be little to choose between the parties on the issue of civil rights. Those who care about this issue before all others would do well to look behind mere party labels in making a choice between two candidates, whether for House, Senate, or Presidency.*

* The major division on this issue during the first seven years of the Eisenhower administration was recorded in the final vote on the modest Civil Rights Act of 1957, which created a Civil Rights Commission to study the problem of discrimination and report its findings, provided for an additional Assistant Attorney General to head a special Civil Rights Division in the Department of Justice, and authorized the Attorney General to seek injunctions in the federal courts to restrain acts of interference with the right to vote. The vote in Congress, which was along sectional rather than party lines, was: in the House, Democrats, for, 128; against, 82 (79 from the South); Republicans, for, 151; against, 15; in the Senate, Democrats, for, 23; against, 15 (all from the South); Republicans, for, 37; against, 0.

According to a "reliable source" available to the *New York Times* (January 22, 1960, and succeeding dates), the party count of names on a petition to dislodge a civil-rights bill from the Rules Committee of the House was Democrats 160, Republicans 30.

A proposal for a constitutional amendment outlawing the poll tax in federal elections and enfranchising residents of the District of Columbia was passed in the Senate February 2, 1960, by a vote of 70 (43 Democrats and 27 Republicans) to 18 (12 Democrats and 6 Republicans). The twelve recalcitrant Democrats were all from the South. Of particular interest is the fact that both senators from Florida, Tennessee, and Texas were recorded in favor of the amendment, as were Senators Long of Louisiana and Jordan of North Carolina.

Almost everything that I have been saying about differences in style, temper, principle, and policy between the parties at the national level applies with equal, perhaps even stronger, force to the parties at the state or local level. Wherever they are in a position to contend fairly equally for control of government, the Democrats, for all their fondness for the middle of the road, are essentially a party of innovation and liberalism, which includes being liberal with other people's money, the Republicans, for all their flashes of insurgency and urges to be "me-tooers," essentially a party of preservation and conservatism. I cannot emphasize strongly enough that Democrats draw more votes than Republicans from people who want government to spend money on them, Republicans more votes than Democrats from people who want government to leave them in possession of the money they have. When it comes to a decisive vote in the legislatures of Illinois, Pennsylvania, or Washington on public housing, mental-health clinics, or unemployment benefits, the Democrats, minus the usual stragglers, will move almost instinctively to one side, the Republicans, minus the usual mavericks, will move even more instinctively to the other. When it comes to a vote on programs to attract new industry or on tax relief in an election year, they will all dance around happily in the center of the stage and make a mockery of my labored attempts to find the difference between them.

I trust that no one will read too much high principle into this liberal-conservative division in our party politics, nor accuse me of celebrating one party as "the good guys" and scorning the other as "the bad guys." Each party's characteristic ism is a practical tendency arising out of the interplay of interests, not a doctrinal stance supported by a series of carefully reasoned principles. One has only to study the activities of Congress in such matters as civil liberties and support of the arts to realize that neither Jefferson nor Burke stalks the halls of Congress, and that the essential Democratic-Republican division is between a visceral, self-serving, bread-and-butter liberalism and a visceral, self-serving, bank-account conservatism.

In the course of the last two chapters we have taken occasional note of the existence of strains within our parties, and now we must examine the condition of each more pointedly for signs of inner distress. It is all very well to talk of the difference between two armies called the Democrats and the Republicans, but when each of the armies acts on many occasions as two or three separate units, with at least one of the units fighting alongside rather than against the enemy, what kind of difference is that? I am not concerned here with the dissensions that must rise and subside and rise again in any human organization as large, and as determined to stay large, as an American party, nor am I too interested in the mutual suspicions of, let us say, those Republicans who are farmers and those who are businessmen or those Democrats whose fathers were in the Irish Brigade and those who celebrate Garibaldi. What I am concerned with is the deep, enduring split in each of our parties that makes it a far more clumsy instrument of purposeful action than critics of our political system would like to see it, and that makes the whole system a far more perplexing phenomenon for all of us to understand.

I begin once again with the Democrats, not simply because their own split has lasted a longer time, but because it seems to be deeper, angrier, and more dangerous than the split in the Republicans. The Democrats are more likely as a matter of course to exhibit signs of strain than are the Republicans. A majority party is almost by definition more volatile than a minority party, and the Democratic style has always been rowdier. As Mr. Dooley said to Mr. Hennessey more than a half-century ago:

No, sir, th' dimmycratic party ain't on speakin' terms with itsilf. Whin ye see two men with white neckties go into a sthreet car an'

set in opposite corners while wan mutthers "Thraiter" an' th'
other hisses "Miscreent" ye can bet they're two dimmycratic leaders thryin' to reunite th' gran' ol' party.[7]

The conflict in the Democratic party, however, cuts much
deeper than that. Looked at through the eye of memory, it
shows itself to be the same conflict that was present in the
birth of the party under Jefferson, Madison, Clinton, and
Burr, the separation of the party under Douglas and Yancey,
and the restoration of the party under Seymour and Pendleton:
the conflict of the urban, immigrant, Catholic, laboring North
and the rural, white, Protestant, planting South. Both the
Democratic North and the Democratic South, to be sure, are
much more complicated phenomena than that. The North
has its own tensions between city and country, farm and factory, Irish and Italian, Protestant and Catholic, businessman
and union worker; the South has come a long way from Jefferson or Calhoun or "Pitchfork Ben" Tillman. Yet the conflict
is still there, unchanging in essence though changing in form,
and it comes down in the end to a division between two
powerful sections that hang together through what seems to
be an outright miracle. It shows up in votes in Congress that
deal with civil rights or labor; it ignites demonstrations on the
floor at every national convention; it prevents final party
unity on almost every issue except the organization of the
House and Senate. The gap between, let us say, Senators
Byrd, Russell, and Talmadge on one hand and Senators
Humphrey, Douglas, and Morse on the other is the widest
in all our politics. One must stand in awe of the forces—
memory, habit, inertia, and vested interest, especially an interest in defeating the Republicans—that keep such men in the
same party.

It may be useful to digress for a few paragraphs on the
subject of the South in American politics. This is one subject, of course, on which we are all experts—with Professors
Key and Heard leading the way [8]—so that much of what I

have to say will be familiar to my readers. Still, it never hurts to look old facts in the face, and these facts have never appeared as solid as they do today.

The eleven states of the old Confederacy—Virginia, North Carolina, South Carolina, Georgia, Florida, Alabama, Tennessee, Mississippi, Arkansas, Louisiana, and Texas—are far and away the most visible, uniform, and powerful sectional unit in American national politics. In six other states on the border —Kentucky, Delaware, Maryland, West Virginia, Missouri, and Oklahoma—Southern sectionalism is an influential if not decisive force.

Although the pattern of internal politics varies from state to state—from the ruthless Byrd machine in Virginia to the "incredibly complex melange of amorphous factions" in Florida by way of a state like Tennessee where the Republicans "approximate the reality of a political party" [9]—all eleven can be classified as one-party states, that is, political communities in which government has been for generations a monopoly of the adherents of one party. In a section of our famously two-party country that holds almost one-quarter of the total population, only one party elects its candidates to national, state, and local office.

The common sign of this one-party system is the emasculation of the machinery of election and its effective replacement by the machinery of nomination, which is, of course, the primary of the dominant party.[10]

This party has been the Democratic party for more than 75 years in some states and a full 150 in others. Except in Tennessee in 1920, no Republican has been elected governor in one of these states since the days of Reconstruction. In the upper houses of the South the Democratic-Republican count is at present 439 to 11, in the lower houses 1,307 to 33. Exactly half this grand total of 44 Republicans is to be found in Nashville; in six of the eleven state capitols there are none at all.

The pattern of Democratic domination is almost as firm at the national level. The South has 106 seats in the House; 99 are occupied by Democrats. (The Republican representation is: Tennessee and Virginia, two each; Texas, North Carolina, and Florida, one each.) It sends 22 senators; all are Democrats, and all have been since time out of mind. Since 1876 five states—Alabama, Arkansas, Georgia, Mississippi, and South Carolina—have never once given their electoral votes to the Republican candidate for the Presidency. Harding carried Tennessee in 1920; Hoover carried Tennessee, Florida, Texas, North Carolina, and Virginia in 1928; Eisenhower carried these states less North Carolina in 1952, the same four plus Louisiana in 1956.

The South is a Democratic citadel because of tradition, vested interest, and the memory of the Civil War and Reconstruction. Even today, except among immigrants from the North and in vestigial enclaves like Winston County in Alabama or Sevier County in Tennessee, it is just not respectable —and can be socially and economically disastrous—to be a "card-carrying" Republican.

The South is a one-party area primarily because of the Negro. In Key's authoritative words:

In its grand outlines the politics of the South revolves around the position of the Negro. It is at times interpreted as a politics of cotton, as a politics of free trade, as a politics of agrarian poverty, or as a politics of planter and plutocrat. Although such interpretations have a superficial validity, in the last analysis the major peculiarities of southern politics go back to the Negro. Whatever phase of the southern political process one seeks to understand, sooner or later the trail of inquiry leads to the Negro.[11]

To be short and blunt about this matter, the Democratic party exercises a near-monopoly of political allegiance in the South because this system appears to be the stoutest bulwark of white supremacy. Whatever differences of class or interest or political principle may divide the white community of the South—and these differences are no less impressive than those that divide men in the North—they are muffled and suppressed and, as it were, sacrificed to unity in the transcendent interest of the whole community in "keeping the Negro in his place." Men carry on their struggles, which can be hot and vicious, within the party. The party itself presents a united face to the rest of the country.

Finally, the strength of the traditional allegiance of most Southerners to the Democratic party makes it impossible for them, even in their hours of galling frustration, to switch this allegiance to the Republicans. A Southerner brought up as a Democrat would find it psychologically almost impossible to join and work for the party of Thaddeus Stevens, and nine out of ten Southerners were brought up as Democrats. The revealing fact of the memorable walkout of Alabama, Mississippi, Louisiana, and South Carolina from the Democratic convention in 1948 was the refusal of the leaders of those four state parties to have anything to do with the Republicans. They would be Dixiecrats, yes, but not Republicans, and in their vocabulary "Dixiecrat" was a synonym for "real Democrat." Significantly, the only states their ticket of Thurmond and Wright carried were those in which they had maneuvered successfully to appropriate the Democratic label.

The Southern Democracy, to be sure, shows some cracks in its supposedly solid façade. The elections of 1928 and 1948 proved, each in its own way, that the South would not swallow "any old candidate" the convention nominated. The last two of Roosevelt's four sweeps of the South were marked by stirrings of "presidential Republicanism," that is, the now settled habit of many conservative Southerners of voting Democratic for every office that appears on the ballot except for the highest office of all. And the spectacular successes of Eisenhower, who twice cut the electorate almost exactly in half, have caused many observers to wonder if the South is not approaching the brink of a political revolution. Yet Eisenhower was Eisenhower, a Texas-born hero who seemed to rise above politics (including Republican politics), and it is doubtful whether any Republican will match his record in the South for years to come. In my final chapter I will speculate about the future of the South, but there is not much speculating to be done about the present. The fact of 1960 is that the South, which becomes more of a minority every year in terms of both interests and numbers, wants to remain Democratic. In the face of the challenge touched off by *Brown* v. *Board of Education,* it has perhaps more reason to be Democratic than it did ten years ago. Its eleven sovereign parties will come to every national convention determined to be loyal Democrats if the other thirty-nine sovereign parties will let them be, and their leaders will go home to sit on their hands or form a transient third party or even work silently for the Republican candidate only if the North (which now stretches to Hawaii) forces an adamant civil-rights plank and an aggressive civil-rights candidate upon the convention.

One never knows what the leaders of the North will do in this matter, for the pressures to be a "truly liberal" party (and thus to write off most of the South) and the temptations to hold on to those 128 "sure" electoral votes (and thus to compromise with it) are both tremendous. The Democrats were able to live fairly comfortably with their historic split in the days of Cleveland and Wilson. Indeed, there were other splits, such as those personified in the enmity of Cleveland and Bryan, that cut much deeper into the party's soul. The coming-and-staying of Franklin Roosevelt changed all that. The New Deal made loyal Democrats of the Negroes of the North, and the party had henceforth to hold their allegiance or risk defeat in a half-dozen key states. The New Deal led the way toward the welfare state, and the party had henceforth to pay special attention to the interests of the urban, working masses. As the party of Northern Negroes, a civil-rights party, it became an affront to the whole South. As the party of organized labor, a high-tax, big-spending, reform-minded party, it became an affront to the conservative South, which is large and powerful. The affront, which Walter Reuther and Adam Clayton Powell would consider mutual, is now a fact of life in Congress. In the jockeying and voting on foreign affairs, defense, the farm problem, and the tariff (although the deviations on this count increase as the South grows more industrial), the Democrats are at least as united a party as the Republicans. On issues like civil rights and regulation of labor, however, they can be counted on to split sharply. The men from Texas and Tennessee, no longer straight-out Southern Democrats, do their best to hammer out workable compromises, and old Democratic hands in both North and South walk as softly as their principles and constituents will let them. But the split is a deep one that must become deeper with the passage of the years, and perhaps it will finally prove too much for both wings to bear. The most important result of this split is the alliance, sometimes shadowy and other times quite substantial, into which it forces conservative Southern Democrats and conservative Northern Republicans in both House and Senate, and some men look forward to the day when this alliance will be the basis of a new party.

This brings us naturally to a survey of the historic split in the Republican party, which also cuts much deeper than the inevitable dissensions between East and West, big business and small business, suburb and county seat. The Republicans began life as a loose coalition of dissenting interests that were united only in their desire to keep slavery out of the territories. In the decade between 1858 and 1868 the men of business rose to a position of ascendancy within the party, and other men, including the progressive-minded politicians who had put the party together in the first place, had to scramble as best they could to win their share of influence and rewards. That early split, which has assumed a half-dozen forms in the course of a century, persists to this day as a fact of life with which the party must contend. In the 1880's it was Stalwarts against Half-Breeds, in the 1900's Regulars against Progressives; today it is the Old Guard against the Modern Republicans. Although it can be explained partly in terms of section, class, and economic interest, at bottom the split in Republicanism is one of principle. It is, in one word, ideological, and the dividing line runs roughly but visibly between those who, like Governor Dewey and the *New York Herald Tribune*, are really quite comfortably at home with the new responsibilities created by Roosevelt and Truman and those who, like Senator Hickenlooper and the *Chicago Tribune*, are not. This split also appears as one between the sophisticated conservatism of corporation executives and the traditional conservatism of small-town leaders.

Most leaders in the party, being politicians in the first place, have been more interested to heal than to exacerbate this split. President Eisenhower, who appears to be a Modern Republican, has reached out steadily to the men on the right. The late Senator Taft, who was the ideal of the Old Guard, always kept a door open to the left. Senator Dirksen has flitted from one camp to the other and back again with each small shift in the prevailing wind. Vice-President Nixon has performed a political miracle in finding glad acceptance on both sides of the line. Republican officeholders and organization men all over the country have submerged their aspirations, whether reactionary or progressive, in an attempt to stay together and thump the Democrats. Yet no one who watches the Republicans go through their paces in Congress and at the nominating convention can fail to detect the two polar urges that separate most of them finally into the new guard and the old or, as I still prefer, into the Half-Breeds and the Stalwarts.

In its present form the Republican split emerged in full view for the first time at the Philadelphia convention of 1940.

Wendell Willkie, a man who had once been a delegate to the Democratic convention, was the force that turned two vague tendencies into two proud camps. The choice of this undoubted Half-Breed, who promised only to be a better, cleaner, more efficient New Dealer than Franklin Roosevelt, over Robert A. Taft, who promised to roll back history at least a couple of years, proved that both progressivism and conservatism were powerful forces in the party, and that any peace between them would always be shaky. It proved, too, although few persons recognized it at the time, that the Republicans would henceforth nominate candidates for the Presidency from the progressive wing or invite disaster. I will have more to say on this point in the final chapter.

Franklin Roosevelt made a reality of the New Economy in the years between 1933 and 1940 and thus contributed importantly to the split that became incarnate in the persons of Willkie and Taft. He and Harry Truman made a reality of the New Diplomacy in the years between 1940 and 1947 and thus contributed almost gleefully to the further split that became incarnate in the persons of Vandenberg and Bricker. The liberal wing of the Republican party, having shouted "Me, too" to social security and T.V.A., now shouted "Me, too" to the U.N., the Truman Doctrine, and NATO. The conservative wing, having winced or even gagged over social security and T.V.A., now winced or gagged over the endless adventures we seemed to be embarking on abroad.[12] I do not wish to give a picture of total antagonism between Republicans who are indistinguishable from left-wing, "globalist" Democrats and Republicans who have not moved an inch beyond Coolidge. Except for a few mavericks like Wayne Morse, who eventually had to cross the aisle, the Modern Republicans have professed a brand of progressivism that is both prudent and modest. Except for a few incorrigibles like Ralph Gwinn, who eventually retired from active politics, the Old Guard Republicans have learned to live in the new world.

Yet there can be no doubt that a wide gap of ideology and aspiration yawns between men like Senators Case of New Jersey, Javits, and Cooper and Senators Goldwater, Capehart, and Bridges. The lofty figure of Eisenhower has kept them all working amiably together, but the split may yet deepen into a serious wound. It will be the constant purpose of the party's "honest brokers," for whom Eisenhower is one kind of model and Dirksen another, to keep this from happening. In the meantime the urge to have less government, lower taxes, and fewer commitments abroad will continue to contest for the soul of the party with the urge to be "creatively conservative," that is, to beat the Democrats to the next series of punches.

Except for small bands of extremists at both ends of both parties, most politically minded Americans seem ready to live with the present situation indefinitely. For mutinous Republicans the outlet to the right is one of the many small ultra-conservative parties that blossom in every election and put up men like General MacArthur or T. Coleman Andrews as candidates for President, to the left the brave course of Senator Morse: a switch to the Democratic party. For mutinous Democrats there are two outlets to the right: presidential Republicanism or a splinter, states-rights party for Southerners; the welcoming arms of the Republican party for Northerners. To the left loom only the ruins of American socialism. Radical politics is in a sorry condition in this country, and the radicals among us must live unhappily with the Democrats or fecklessly amid the ruins. To tell the truth, insurgency is out of style.

One reason for the present strength of the two major parties, by which I mean the remarkable capacity of each to keep its own peculiar split from widening disastrously, is the interesting modus vivendi under which Congress, during the past few generations, has become the special preserve of the conservatives in both parties and the Presidency the special preserve of the progressives. The causes of this situation lie deep in our institutions and habits, and they may well prevail for some time to come.

The first cause would surely be the dual electoral process outlined in the Constitution and the practices we have grafted onto it. We elect the Congress under a system that is gerrymandered by design and inertia in favor of rural, small-state, and thus more conservative interests,[13] the President under a system that is gerrymandered by the exclusive use of the general ticket * in favor of urban, large-state, and thus more progressive interests. A second cause is the practices of the parties, each of which has come in its own way to recognize that it must nominate a progressive candidate for the Presidency or hazard a crushing defeat, and each of which leaves the choice of candidates for the House and Senate entirely in the hands of state and local organizations. A third is the independent habits of American voters, millions of whom seem quite prepared to choose one kind of man to represent their more parochial interests on Capitol Hill and another to represent their broader interests in the White House. A fourth is what we might call "the imperatives of the Presidency." The very nature of the office, especially as our chosen instrument of diplomacy and defense, forces men who hold it to adopt a more active posture toward the world and its problems. However strong and sincere Senator Taft's urges toward isolation, it is hard to imagine his acting too much differently from Eisenhower if he had managed to win the Presidency.

A final cause, about which millions of words are written and spoken fruitlessly every year, is the rules and customs of Congress. Thanks to the seniority system, which is a product primarily of custom, the House and Senate are led by men who are returned again and again from safe districts.[14] Such men, if they are Democrats, are mostly from the South and

---

* I refer to the fact that in each of the fifty states (and by the free choice of those states) the electoral vote goes in one lump to the presidential candidate with a plurality in the popular vote.

the border states, although a few do slip in from the urban North. Such men, if they are Republicans, are mostly from small towns and small states. In the present Senate, for example, the chairmen of eight of the ten most important committees come from the Confederacy. Whatever else they may be, Senators Russell, Robertson, Byrd, and Eastland are not Democrats with a progressive cast of mind—nor, it seems clear, are they likely candidates for the Presidency. In the last House to be controlled by the Republicans (1953–1954), the chairmen of all twelve of the most important committees came from stanchly Republican districts in places like Kansas, Michigan, Nebraska, upstate New York, and downstate Illinois. Whatever else they may have been, Representatives Taber, Reed of New York, McConnell, Hoffman, Allen, and Velde were not exactly Modern Republicans. They were all, if anything, well to the right of Senator Taft. Neither Modern Republicans nor liberal Democrats, most of whom come from marginal districts where the tides of politics ebb and flow, are a consistently vital factor in the leadership of Congress. The rules and customs, I repeat, are loaded against them, not only the seniority rule, but also such bulwarks of the conservative cause as the filibuster in the Senate and the inordinate power of the Rules Committee in the House.

The truth is that at the national level each party is really two parties: a party that controls the convention and nominates men of progressive instinct or appearance for the Presidency, and a party that, having lost effective control of the convention years ago, still manages very nicely to exercise conservative leadership in Congress. There are, to be sure, many ties between the party temporarily in command of the White House and the party with the same name in Congress. (The party not in command of the White House, which is currently the presidential party of the Democrats, is always in a state of suspended animation until the next convention meets.) A President, whether Democratic or Republican, will temper many demands in his program to the mood of his allies in Congress. The leaders of the party in Congress, who can feel the pressure of the White House, will try to suppress their conservative urges and honor the President's sensible requests. There is nonetheless a constant tension between the two Democratic parties, which is matched by a tension between the two Republican parties. Both are projections of those celebrated splits with which our parties have been living for generations.

Where, then, is the heart of each party, and what is the distance between dead-center Republicanism and dead-center Democracy? The answer, I think, is that the heart of the Republican party is that position where Senator Taft pitched his famous camp—halfway between the standpattism of "the unreconstructed Old Guard" and the me-tooism of "the disguised New Dealers." The heart of the Democratic party, at least in thirty-nine states of the Union, is that position where Adlai Stevenson raised his famous standard—halfway between the aggressive reformism of "the laboristic liberals" and the moderate opportunism of "the Texas brokers." Neither of these notable men could win through to the Presidency and thus put his mark indelibly on his party. Taft, indeed, was too good a Republican even to win the nomination. Yet each in his own way and at his best moments came as close to being the beau ideal of his party as did any man in the postwar years.

The distance between the well-known positions of these two men on domestic and international affairs is a pretty accurate measure of the distance between the two parties and as reasonable an answer as one can make to those who still demand to know "the difference between the Democrats and the Republicans." The difference, I repeat, is one of tendencies rather than principles. In most parts of this country it comes down to a difference between an urban, working-class, new-stock, union-oriented party with a penchant for reform and spending, and a rural-suburban, middle-class, old-stock, business-oriented party with a penchant for the status quo and saving. Look deep into the soul of a Democrat and you will find plans to build 400,000 units of public housing and to ship 300 tractors to Ghana (whether Ghana wants them or not); look deep into the soul of a Republican and you will find hopes for a reduction in taxes and for a balanced budget.

There are those who will insist that this is not enough of a difference. Each of the parties is a permissive coalition within which the basic urges of the heart are too often sacrificed on the altar of a specious unity. Each overlaps the other excessively in principle, aspiration, and appeal; each abandons its alleged identity in the scramble for votes. And in each may be found, even in states where the Republican-Democratic split is sharpest, important men who seem to vote more often with the other party than with their own, for example, Senator Lausche of Ohio and Senator Javits of New York. To persons who complain on all these scores I can say only that those are the facts of life in a two-party system that operates under a constitution of divided authority. A party that presumes to be a majority must of necessity be a coalition; two parties that are locked in equal struggle must of necessity overlap. Let the critics of the American parties go to any other country with two-party politics, even to relatively homogeneous Britain, and there, too, they will see evidences of internal compromise and external overlap; there, too, they will hear complaints about the lack of clear-cut differences between the parties.[15] This is the burden of the citizen of such a country, and especially of the United States: never to be sure of the "real difference" between the two parties, never to be certain that his vote will "count," always to be on the alert for maverick candidates, always to look beneath party labels at the men who wear them.

If my readers have learned from this chapter to bear this

burden a bit more easily, I shall be content. If they still refuse
to acknowledge the differences between the Democrats and
the Republicans, I shall be forced to conclude that, at least
for them, there are none.*

* It may be of interest to note that, according to long-range studies
by the Roper Center at Williams College, "a consistent majority—at times
as high as two-thirds to three-quarters—of the adult population of the
United States perceives a clear distinction in ideological and interest-
group propensity between the two major parties. The polls tend to
verify the commonly accepted caricature that the Democratic Party is
the party of the poor and of labor and the Republican Party is the
party of business and of the rich. In the field of foreign policy the public
sees little difference between the parties, although at times it has given
a slight edge to the Republican Party as the more successful avoider of
open combat. These stereotypes may be less important as accurate de-
scriptions of party differences than as reflections of the public's belief
that the parties actually provide meaningful alternatives in many areas
of policy, even though there are important areas of consensus."

Perceptions of party differences are, of course, an important factor in
our political system, since the label a candidate bears can be a decisive
determinant of his and his constituency's voting behavior.[16]

V

The Future of American Politics

SOME skeptical readers may feel that the title of this chapter makes a questionable assumption: that American politics has a future. What certainty do we have, they may ask perversely, that the politics of compromise, moderation, pragmatism, overlapping, give-and-take, mutual confidence, and group diplomacy will last more than a few years in the ever more savage world and ever more frantic society into which we seem to be heading? What right have we to assume that the future of the American party system will be a natural extension of its extraordinary past?

No more certainty and no better right, I would answer, than we have to assume that American democracy itself has a future, at least enough of a future to keep us working, planning, and dreaming as we always have in this country. If our democracy does have such a future, and surely it does, then our politics, too, will continue to prosper as it has prospered in the past. It may in time become more principled and disciplined. It may be directed toward ends far different from those it served under the guidance of Jefferson, Lincoln, Wilson, and Eisenhower, and of John Beckley, Thurlow Weed,

Mark Hanna, and James A. Farley. Yet it will still be a politics in the American style, and we will be able to judge the condition of our democracy in the condition of our politics. I must repeat again my conviction that parties are useful, effective, and altogether indispensable instruments of constitutional democracy. A country like the United States, Great Britain, or Sweden might wish or even choose to swap one kind of party system for another, but it could never wish or choose, not while it remained a constitutional democracy, to proceed on its way with no party system at all. The essence of democracy is politics, and politics without parties in a widespread and diverse community is really not politics at all.

Since American politics appears to have a future, we must do what we can to look into that future and see what it may hold for us. I propose to do this by peering down each of the two sights along which men are accustomed to take aim on the future: prediction and prescription. I want to talk first about what is likely to happen on the American political scene in the next generation—between now and 1984—and second about what ought to happen. My predictions will be those of a political historian who seeks to project present trends as objectively as he can into a future whose outlines are already visible. My prescriptions will be those of a political scientist who perhaps finds more reason in the American party system than do many of his fellow citizens, and who is not generally disposed, certainly not in the real world of people and institutions, to advocate abrupt changes in traditional ways of doing the public business. I think it only fair to warn my readers, as if they could not guess, that this chapter is the work of one who has a considerable if not exactly uncritical affection and admiration for the American political system.

Before we can look ahead to the politics of 1984, we ought to take notice of the politics of the immediate future, which comes every year for our two great parties. What concerns them is not the next generation but the next election. This obsessive concentration on the immediate future may be unfortunate, but it is clearly the way of practical politics; and that is the kind of politics we play in this country. To create an electoral majority rather than doctrinal unity, to win power rather than to use it, has been the consuming purpose of American parties.

Our parties are concerned about all elections they must fight, but it is the one that comes every fourth year that really rouses them to action. Hamilton engaged in one of his keenest displays of prophecy when he foretold a time "when every vital question of state will be merged in the question, 'who will be the next President?'" That time has come, and it is a time that has no end. The next election for President now begins the day the last election ends, and for our parties this means that the future is always on top of them.

In rousing the parties from idle speculation to determined action, the presidential election also makes them, as much as they ever can be in our federal system, national parties. The importance of the Presidency, that compelling focus of power, prestige, and patronage, for the character and very existence of our parties is beyond all calculation. Arthur Macmahon comes close to the truth of the matter when he observes that the major parties "may be described as loose alliances to win the stakes of power embodied in the Presidency." [1] The one persistent purpose for the existence of an American party on a national scale, the one force that creates even a loose alliance out of fifty grand duchies and hundreds of petty baronies, is to elect a President. In the nominating convention the national party springs suddenly to life, and for the next three or four months it almost looks like an organization set up to operate effectively throughout the land. Then, when the election is over, it disintegrates into its hundreds of sovereign components. They fight their parochial elections without much regard for one another and wait for the day when the enormous magnet of the Presidency draws them once again into an army which, if not highly disciplined, at least marches more or less in the same direction.

The immediate future of each party, then, appears in the form of a fascinating problem—to find a man who can capture the White House under its banner, if not necessarily in pursuit of all its principles. Let us look at the process through which the Democrats and Republicans go about solving this problem, for in so doing we can learn a great deal about some of their common characteristics and special quirks. I must assume that my readers already know something of the timetable and rituals of a presidential canvass—how we move step by step through the early stages of hat tossing, the pre-primary campaigns, the state primaries and conventions and committee meetings, the national conventions, the campaign, the plebiscite, the meeting of the electoral colleges, and so on to the last formality of counting the electoral vote and proclaiming the winner. What I am interested in expounding are the rules that seem to govern each party's pursuit of glory, and that lead it to choose a certain type of man as its candidate for President and to shun many other types.

First, let us take note of the tests that must be met by all persons who are recommended or recommend themselves for nomination by either of the major parties. Not all of them are polite or even reasonable; many of them smell of prejudice and vulgarity. They are nonetheless the unwritten laws of presidential "availability," the best answers I can make to the hard questions: What kind of man can be nominated for President of the United States? What kind of man cannot hope to be nominated? We are not dealing here with the qualities a man must have or cultivate if he is to be an effective President, but rather with the attributes he must have (many of them impossible to cultivate) before he has a right to think of being President at all. We are no less concerned with those attributes—ethnic, religious, geographic, cultural, physical, social—that disqualify a man no matter how eminent and talented a person he may be.

Let me answer the questions in the form of a list that may not seem scientific but is loaded with fact.[2] If my reading of American history and understanding of American values is at all correct, then we may say of a man who thirsts for the Presidency:

First, he must be, according to the Constitution, at least thirty-five years old, a "natural born" citizen, and "fourteen years a resident within the United States."

Second, he must be, according to unwritten law, white, male, and Christian.

Third, he almost certainly must be less than sixty-five years old, a Northerner or Westerner, of northern European stock, and healthy.

Fourth, he ought to be, according to the historic tests of availability, more than forty-five years old, from a state larger than Kentucky, a family man, of British stock, a veteran, a Protestant, a lawyer, a joiner, a small-town boy, a self-made man (especially if a Republican), and a cultural middle-brow.

Fifth, it appears to make no difference whether he is a college graduate, a small businessman, a state governor, a member of Congress, a member of the Cabinet, or a defeated candidate for the Presidency—providing that he emerged from his defeat the very image of the happy warrior.

Sixth, he ought not to be, again according to the tests of availability, from a state smaller than Kentucky, divorced, a bachelor, a Catholic, a former Catholic, a corporation president, a twice-defeated candidate for the Presidency, an intellectual, a professional soldier, a professional politician, or conspicuously rich.

Seventh, he almost certainly cannot be a Southerner,* of

---

* For more reasons than one, I am not entirely certain whether Texas is in the South or West, but I think it is still enough of a Southern state

Polish, Italian, or Slavic stock, a union official, or an ordained minister.

Eighth, he cannot be, according to unwritten law, a Negro, a Jew, an Oriental, a woman, or an atheist.

Ninth, he cannot be, according to the Constitution, a former President with more than a term and one-half of service,* less than thirty-five years old, a naturalized citizen, or an expatriate.

Several things should be noted about this list. First, I have purposely left out a number of intangibles—moral repute, presence, eloquence, intelligence, moderation in views and tastes, willingness to run hard and to serve faithfully, the look of a winner—that are factors of decisive importance in transforming men who are merely available into serious contenders for nomination. What I have tried to list are those self-evident qualifications and disqualifications which dry up the pool of available men to probably not more than a hundred Americans. Second, any rule in the fourth and sixth categories can be broken with relative impunity by an eminent man who scores high on the other tests of availability. Wendell Willkie was a corporation president, Adlai Stevenson was divorced, William Jennings Bryan was a twice-defeated candidate, Al Smith was a Catholic, yet they were nominated by hardheaded politicians who expected them to win. None of them did win, be it remembered, and we may conclude that each of them lost a sizable number of votes by reason of his particular disqualification. Third, the rules do not apply quite so rigidly to aspirants for the Vice-Presidency. No man born and living in the South has been nominated for the Presidency on a major party ticket since Zachary Taylor in 1848, but the nomination of John Sparkman of Alabama in 1952 is proof that the Democrats will give second place on their ticket to a man ineligible for

---

to make the nomination of one of its sons a practical impossibility. I could be wrong.

* Unless his name is Harry S. Truman, the one American to whom Amendment xxii does not apply.

first. So, too, will the Republicans, who certainly would not have nominated a man as young as Richard Nixon for President in 1952, but who gave freshness to their ticket by putting him up for Vice-President. One of these days we may even see a woman in second place on the ticket of a major party.

I cannot guarantee the applicability of every item on this list, especially those in the middle categories, any longer than the next quarter-century. Although many of our tastes and common expectations (and, alas, our prejudices) are constant to the point of obduracy, at least a few are likely to change, as they have changed in the past, under the pressures of social progress and readjustment. If men of Italian or Polish descent are not eligible today, they may be in the year 2000. Catholics were not eligible in 1900, but they have become more eligible with every new census of religious affiliation in the United States. Indeed, we may have reached the point at which a party, especially the Democratic party, would hurt itself more by refusing nomination to a Catholic who had a commanding popular lead and was otherwise fully available than by defying an ancient taboo that is slowly losing its force. Assuming that their other qualifications are identical, however, a Protestant is still more likely than a Catholic to be nominated and elected President.

This list says almost nothing about achievement, experience, and national reputation, and I must hasten to add that these, too, are tests that every candidate must pass. The days of William H. Harrison, Warren G. Harding, and perhaps even Wendell Willkie—the days of the dark horse or the fourth-rate compromise or the comet—are gone forever. The electorate has labored through a demanding course in history and politics in the past generation, and it has learned to ask for big men in its biggest office. It wants a choice between candidates who are not merely attractive and available, but talented and tested. No weaklings, ciphers, and men of local reputation need apply, nor men who promise only to be meek and mild. The Presidency will henceforth be reserved for men who are or appear to be—we can always be fooled—strong and experienced. The kind of experience that we are most likely to demand of each candidate is the kind that will make him a match, not so much for Rayburn and Faubus and Hoffa, but for Khrushchev and Nehru and De Gaulle. More and more we are coming to regard the Presidency as a mighty weapon in the struggle for power among nations rather than a blue chip in the game of preferment among Americans. Partisan considerations loom perhaps less prominently in the election of a President than they do in the election of almost any other major official or legislator in our national, state, and city governments.

In addition to these general considerations that apply almost equally to both parties, there are others of a special nature that apply forcefully to only one. Each party, that is to say, has its own peculiar problem to solve in the course of its search for a winning candidate. The problem of the Democrats stems from the fact, which I have documented in earlier chapters, that it is the majority party in the country, the problem of the Republicans from the related fact that it is the minority party. The problem of each is made real and challenging by the further fact of the restlessness and independence of a sizable part of the American electorate. All other things being equal, as I also said before, the Democrats should win every national election, but "things" are far more likely to be "equal" in a congressional than in a presidential election. Political habits and allegiances mean much less than usual, personalities and issues much more, in the race for the grand prize of American politics.

The special problem of the Democratic party is to mobilize its majority, that is, to nominate a candidate for the Presidency who can bring the party's own voters in droves to the polls. If it is important to find a man who can appeal to the floaters in the center and to the deviants in the Republican party, it is even more important to find one who can hold together the squabbling legions of this amazing coalition, who can please both the United Automobile Workers and the United Daughters of the Confederacy, the Irish of Boston and the Jews of Brooklyn, the professors and the professionals, the farmers and the factory workers, the white supremacists of Georgia and the Negroes of Harlem. This is a task not easily accomplished, especially now that the issue of civil rights is out in the open where it belongs. Still, the Democrats have a long history of successful group diplomacy, and a little thing like getting Herman Talmadge and Adam Clayton Powell to lie down together is not going to stand in the way of their quest for victory. In the conventions of the future, as in those of the past, the Democrats can be expected to come up with an experienced, appealing, available candidate who meets three special standards that are inherent in the nature and situation of the party:

First, he must be a loyal son of the party, a warrior with stars on his campaign ribbons and scars on his body. The Democrats, who are perhaps more intense in their loyalty than the Republicans (and less pressed to woo the independent vote), are less likely to go running after generals and recent converts.

Second, he must not be openly hostile to any one of the major elements in the great coalition. Indeed, he should have proved himself to be at least an understanding listener to the woes of Negroes, states-righters, union leaders, immigrants, and small farmers well before he betrays an interest in the Presidency.

And third, he must not be too closely identified with any one of these elements. As he cannot be a Southerner, lest Northern liberals "wave the bloody shirt" at him, so he should not be a man of the city machine, lest he remind the South of Al Smith. As he cannot be a Pole, Italian, Jew, Negro, white supremacist, union official, or professional civil-libertarian, so he should not be a Roman Catholic or an intellectual.

To get down to cases, the Democrats, even when they were stuck fast in a minority position, paid homage to the unwritten laws of the party, which until 1936 were given written support in the form of the famous two-thirds rule. The nomination of every candidate from George B. McClellan through John W. Davis was the result of a grand exercise in self-conscious group diplomacy. The nomination of Al Smith in 1928, however, was a violation of the unwritten laws of the old Democracy on at least three if not four counts,* and the new Democracy paid for it in the unprecedented loss of five states in the South to a stalwart Republican. The nomination of someone like Senator Glass of Virginia, I suspect, would have been even more disastrous.

The party returned to the ancient ways of compromise in the four nominations of Roosevelt and in the choice of Harry S. Truman (instead of either James F. Byrnes or Henry Wallace) for Vice-President in 1944. The nomination of Truman in 1948, which was made doubly unpalatable to the South by the civil-rights plank in the party's platform, put a strain on the unwritten laws,† but this strain was more than mitigated four years later by the nomination of Adlai Stevenson. If anyone doubts the force of the laws I have been discussing, let him try to account in any other way for the choice in the convention of 1952 of this reluctant man: not a Southerner but blessed with friends and relations in the South, not a "labor-liberal" but owning a record of sympathy toward unions, not a product of urban politics but able to find his way around Chicago, not a Catholic but also not a belligerent

---

* In those days the split of Wets and Drys presented an additional problem in group diplomacy to the Democratic professionals.

† Yet it was also a confirmation of the force of these laws. As Samuel Lubell has pointed out, the "unanimity" of the Democratic leaders "in desiring to get rid of Truman was surpassed only by their inability to agree on anyone to take his place." [3]

Protestant, not a Jew or a professor or a professional or a second-generation immigrant but a man who counted such people among his closest colleagues, above all not a man who could be identified with any particular calling—and who had that aristocratic background and bearing for which the sweaty Democrats have a startling weakness. If Stevenson had been from Missouri, had served a few years as senator or Secretary of Defense, and had not been divorced, he would have been the almost perfect candidate of the modern Democratic party.

The trouble was, of course, that he ran head on into the perfect candidate of the Republican party—and in a year when, because of "Communism, Corruption, and Korea," all other things were far from being equal. The special problem of the Republicans is to nominate a candidate who can bring the party's voters to the polls and, further, attract several million persons who normally vote Democratic or not at all. A man like Eisenhower was designed in heaven for just such a purpose,[4] and surely there was something a little unreal about the savagery of the struggle between the Eisenhower and Taft forces at the Chicago convention. If Senator Taft had been as good a Democrat as he was a Republican, he would have been nominated for the Presidency at least twice in his life. Unfortunately for him, he was almost too good a Republican, and he went down more than twice to a preordained defeat because his party was driven by the logic of its minority position to seek a candidate with more appeal for that curse of all Stalwarts, the independent vote. So long as the tides of politics run as they are running today, the Republicans choose suicide if they choose a man from the Old Guard. In a career replete with astounding successes Richard Nixon scored the most astounding of all in convincing both the professionals and the voters of his party that he was a Stalwart and something more, that he could rally the whole party and attract several million independents and Democrats in addition. The imperatives that have led the Republicans ever since 1936 to choose Half-Breeds like Willkie, Dewey, and Eisenhower are still strong, and one would have expected Nelson Rockefeller to be the most formidable of challengers. Nixon, however, crushed the opposition to his nomination, not merely by serving Eisenhower imaginatively and the party doggedly, but by convincing the Modern Republicans of Madison Avenue that he was every bit as "liberal" and "internationalist" as Rockefeller. Since he also managed to convince the Old Guard of a thousand Main Streets that he was the legitimate heir of Robert A. Taft, he must be given credit, I repeat, for a brilliant political achievement.

Let me conclude this survey of the immediate future with a tribute to that most exciting of our national rituals, the election of a President of the United States. It is, truly, a wonderful event, one that mixes high drama and low comedy, grand purpose and petty politics, mass persuasion and individual choice, in a collective experience that is uniquely American in character and deeply democratic in spirit. It lasts too long, it costs too much, it makes fools of otherwise sensible men; and it throws our politicians, in Auden's words, into much too "friendly terms with guys in advertising firms." Yet it does the job that must be done in the way in which most Americans want it to be done, and in doing the job so colorfully and well it makes us, paradoxically, a more united people than we are at any other time in the normal course of American events. Without it we would have a far different political system; without it we would find the challenge of nationhood far more difficult to meet. I go most of the way with Professor Binkley, who wonders "how else the electorate as a whole could be made so acutely aware of the very existence of our national state," and all the way with Walt Whitman, who wrote in *Democratic Vistas*, "I know nothing grander, better exercise, better digestion, more positive proof of the past, the triumphant result of faith in human kind, than a well-contested American national election." [5] The

American people are rightly convinced that they have no more solemn task to perform and melodrama to enjoy than to elect their President every four years. It is time they acknowledged the dominant role the parties play in making this crazy-quilt system of election work as well as it does—and that, on any realistic view of the candidates of the past thirty years, is very well indeed.

To return to our survey of the more distant future, it takes very little bravery or insight to predict that, barring a nuclear catastrophe that would leave anarchy or autocracy in its wake, American politics in 1984 will look much like American politics in 1960. If, as I insisted at the end of Chapter II, "*these* parties were designed prescriptively to serve the purposes of *this* people under the terms of *this* Constitution," then there would have to be radical changes in our national character or in our form of government before we could expect any radical changes in our political system.

Such changes do not appear to be in the offing. It is a popular and curiously comforting thing to say that we live in an age of transition, even of revolution, but when have Americans not lived in such an age? If all the vast economic and social strides of the past fifty years brought only a few alterations in our political system, how can we expect the strides of the next generation to bring many more? Whatever new trends are under way in the pattern of our values, purposes, and prejudices, they are not nearly massive enough to alter our ancient attitudes toward politics, especially to broaden or contract substantially the range of our expectations of government. Whatever moving about we do, whether horizontally from place to place or vertically from class to class, we could hardly move any farther or faster than we have moved already in this century. And however many new commitments are made by the national, state, and local governments, they are not likely to put us in any more experimental a political mood than we are in today. Although the Constitution may be stretched here and twisted there in the next generation, just as it has been in the last, its principal features —the separation of powers, federalism, the system of presidential and congressional elections, the fierce independence of Congress, and the ascendant Presidency—will persist in much their present form and work much their present influence on our political folkways. All in all, we have every right to expect the two-party system to endure in unreconstructed glory and the parties themselves to display the time-tested characteristics which I summed up on page 37. As far as my own weak eyes can see into the future, the parties look like the parties of today—loose, supple, overlapping, decentralized, undisciplined, interest-directed, and principle-shunning enterprises in group diplomacy that are encircled and penetrated by a vigorous array of interest groups. They will be, in short, what they have always been—parties that aspire seriously to majority rule in a vast and motley democracy.

Let me come at this fearless prediction from the other side of the problem by painting a black future for third parties. There exist in this country today the materials—substantial materials in the form of potential leaders, followers, funds, interests, and ideological commitments—for at least three important third parties, any one of which could, under the rules of some other system, cut heavily and permanently into the historic Democratic-Republican monopoly. There is no reasonable expectancy, under the rules of our system, that any such party could make a respectable showing in two successive elections. Indeed, if a new third party were to make such a showing in just one election, the major party closest to it would move awkwardly but effectively to absorb it.* I speak, of course, of (1) the white South, which, mobilized

---

* Or even a threat of such a showing. The success of the leftward movement of the Democrats in 1936 (against Long and then Lemke) and 1948 (against Henry Wallace's Progressives) makes discouraging reading for those with hopes for a radical third party.

as an independent force in pursuit of its One Great Interest, might hold the balance of political power in the United States for a generation or more; (2) the non-Communist, politically oriented left (centered principally on the C.I.O. side of that weird combination, the A.F.L.-C.I.O.), which erupts from time to time with threats of a labor-liberal party *—and then subsides into its normal state of being half-master, half-thrall of the Democratic party; and (3) the ultraconservative right, which has the funds and the ideological commitment and would follow Douglas MacArthur to the ends of the earth if his trumpet would only give off a "certain sound." In most other countries these groups, each of which counts its potential supporters in the millions, would have long since formed parties of consequence. In this country they are doomed to frustration, a condition for which most of us, I suspect, are ready to give "much thanks."

Not every facet of our politics will remain exactly as it is today through the next quarter-century. Several trends that are already visible will continue to run their ponderous course and may even run more strongly. The shift from intensely sectional to loosely national politics is still under way. The most obdurate pockets of one-party ascendancy are slowly being eroded, and now that Vermont has elected a Democrat to Congress, who knows what other sanctuaries may give way under the pressure of this trend? It is being helped along, paradoxically, by the continued activity of interest groups. In the words of the Committee on Political Parties of the American Political Science Association:

In one respect the growth of the modern interest groups is exerting a direct effect upon the internal distribution of power within the

---

* Walter Reuther, in particular, sounds the call that was sounded most clearly years ago by that half-forgotten philosopher, archy the cockroach:

    Announcer: Do you think the time is ripe for launching a third national political party in America?

    archy   it is more than ripe it is rotten

parties. They counteract and offset local interests; they are a nationalizing influence. Indeed, the proliferation of interest groups has been one of the factors in the rise of national issues because these groups tend to organize and define their objectives on a national scale.[6]

The shift of millions of Americans from a politics of strong commitment to a politics of perverse independence is also far from completed. It may be true, as some observers have predicted, that we are ready to look with equanimity upon a more or less permanent division of control at the national level, with one party holding the Presidency and the other holding at least one house of Congress. It is certainly true that the professionals in both our parties must be prepared to live with the fact of a restless electorate, and thus to place more emphasis in campaigns on techniques of "conversion" rather than of "activation" and "re-enforcement." [7] Sharper swings and bigger landslides may become the normal pattern of elections in the future. At the same time the influence of class on political behavior and allegiance may become even more visible than it is today, especially as the influences of ethnology and religion fade ever so slowly but steadily from view. As I wrote in Chapter III, we are still a long way from the class struggle in American politics, but that does not mean that class consciousness is a negligible factor. To the contrary, it must inevitably become a more important factor as Americans become ever more alert to the rewards and symbols of status.[8]

Yet even these trends are not powerful enough to alter the basic pattern of American politics. The only large feature of that familiar pattern which I find hard to project confidently into the next twenty-five years is the present majority-minority relationship of the Democrats and the Republicans. I am speaking here, let it be recalled, not of the betting odds in any particular election, but of the long-term political habits and preferences of the American people. Since the early days of the New Deal these have been weighted noticeably in favor of the Democrats. In the congressional elections of 1958, "things" were perhaps as "equal" as they ever can be in our system, by which I mean that the pluses and minuses of such crosscutting forces as issues and personalities worked to cancel one another out and thus to leave each party in possession of its "normal" quota of voters, give or take a few hundred thousand. The total vote for the House of Representatives in that election was: Democrats, 25,641,104, Republicans, 19,763,773. Outside the South the count was 22,816,060 to 19,166,960. This may not be an exact measurement of the degree of Democratic ascendancy, but it is as exact as any we are likely to get. The question is whether it will continue to hold in the future.

Several developments in both the demography and practices of our politics have led tough-minded Republicans to predict their party's recapture of its old majority position within the next decade. Among these are (1) the continuing rise in income, status, education, average age, and proportion of women to men * in the American electorate, all of which are forces that are known or alleged to push voters gently toward the respectable conservatism of the Republicans; (2) the growth of the suburb as a steady counterpoise to the Democratic city and to the increasingly unpredictable country; (3) the mighty image of Dwight D. Eisenhower as the Man of Peace, which could fog the mighty image of Franklin D. Roosevelt as the Man of the People; (4) the growing habit of many Southerners of voting Republican in presidential elections; (5) the new determination of many leaders of business to engage actively in politics; (6) the increasing irritation of small businessmen, farmers, and other "plain people" over the intrusion of organized labor into politics; (7) the possibility that the organization of American workers into unions may have reached the

---

* By 1980, according to the Census Bureau, eligible women (eligible for voting, that is, not for marriage) will exceed eligible men by 5.5 million.

saturation point, and that, in any case, a healthy fraction of these workers will always vote Republican no matter how heavily their leaders swing to the Democrats; and (8) above all the deep-seated conservatism of a nation that has much to preserve—the dollar, for instance—in the face of ill-digested reforms and careless spending. All these forces and trends, it is argued persuasively, are working powerfully toward a reversal of the present standings of the two parties in the hearts of the great American electorate.

Yet it is also argued persuasively, and not just by wishful-thinking Democrats, that the Republicans are doomed to remain a minority for many years to come.[9] Those who predict the continuation of Democratic supremacy make much of the theory of cycles in American politics and attitudes. If the Republicans had forty years of supremacy, surely the Democrats should be able to count on at least fifty. If the swing to conservatism after World War II failed to erase the Democratic edge, surely the coming swing back to liberalism—I am reporting what I have been told, not making any prediction of my own—should make that edge even sharper. In the next generation, the argument runs, more Americans will choose consciously for "the party of creative progress" than for "the party of reluctant acquiescence." These observers also make much of the fact that education can cut both ways, that it can stimulate interest among nonvoters at the lower levels of American society just as easily as it can sustain old voters at the middle and upper levels. Indeed, has it ever been proved that the single factor of education, isolated from such factors as status and income, pushes Americans toward the Republican party? If the "egghead vote" is any evidence, quite the reverse is true. As for increased activity among the more fortunate members of American society, partisans of the Democracy delight in quoting George Meany:

Business is going to go into politics now because of the threat of big labor. Well, all I can say is: "Welcome, come in, the water is fine." Let them go in.

The more they get in with their financial resources, the greater interest they will stir up among the workers, and maybe it will help us get more workers in doing their real duty as citizens.

And when they get down to that contest between workers and big business, we will do all right because there are a little more of us than there are of them.[10]

There are still other points that can be made in support of the expectation of continuing Democratic supremacy. The steady migration of Negroes to the North and the dogged rise in Negro registration in the South promise welcome additions to the Democratic bulge—welcome, in any case, to the party in the North and West. The attack on rural over-representation may yet succeed in correcting some of the most flagrant inequities, and the Democratic cities would stand to gain handsomely from any such successes. The Democrats have many more safe seats in Congress than do the Republicans; any Republican majority in the two houses would, as Lubell notes, be "subject to quick overturning by a counter-swing in relatively few districts." [11] And surely, as Meany pointed out, the "masses" will outnumber the "classes." For all these reasons, I think it fair to predict that the Democrats, if they can keep from exploding, will continue to ride high for several decades. This does not mean, I repeat, that they can count on winning every election. It does mean that they enjoy enough of a head start over the Republicans to enable them to keep control of one or both houses of Congress and of well over half of our state governments for some time to come. It should also enable them to capture the Presidency more often than not—unless, of course, chance continues to deal aces to the Republicans and only face cards to them.

This prediction of continued Democratic ascendancy is all very well, especially for the Democrats, but what about the question posed in the middle of the last paragraph: Can the party of Humphrey, Stevenson, Walter, De Sapio, Lehman, Powell, Byrd, Truman, Arvey, Butler, Eastland, Talmadge, and Farley keep from exploding? To answer that question we must look again to the South, for in the rising tension between the embattled white supremacists of the Confederacy and the minority-conscious politicians of the North and West lies the dynamite that may yet blow the Democracy sky-high. The leaders of the party need lose only a little sleep over the other tensions that are advertised loudly wherever two or three Democrats are gathered together. These tensions—for example, between farmers and union workers or Irish and Italians or professors and professionals—are certainly no more acute than those which keep the Republicans hopping. They are, after all, the burden that any party must carry cheerfully if it aspires to victory in the game of politics as played in this country.

But the split between the eleven Democratic parties of the South (or should we subtract Tennessee and Texas and put the recalcitrants at nine?) and the thirty-nine of the North and West (perhaps less Kentucky and Oklahoma) cuts far more deeply.[12] It was a hard enough thing for the Democrats to live with this split in the days of Cleveland or Wilson or Franklin Roosevelt; in these days it has taxed their powers of ingenuity and intramural forgiveness right up to the limit. The emergence of the Northern Democrats as the party of agitation and reform, the dogged resistance of Southern industry to unionization of its working force, the swing of an increasingly industrialized South toward protectionism and thus a posture of mild isolationism, the inordinate power of the Southern Democrats in Congress and their alliance of convenience with the conservative Republicans, the growing intransigence on each side of the mighty conflict over civil rights and desegregation—all these trends and forces are driving the wedge ever deeper into the immemorial rift in the party of Jefferson and Burr. Burr could forgive Jefferson his slaves; Jefferson could forget his agrarian prejudices for the sake of Burr's support. But how long can Senator Douglas and

Senator Byrd or Walter Reuther and Eugene ("Bull") Connor or Mrs. Roosevelt of New York and Mrs. Fletcher Gore of Mississippi forgive and forget? Almost every Northern Democrat with whom I have talked in the past few years agrees that the future of the party in his area lies in a steady commitment to internationalism, reasonably firm pressure for civil rights and desegregation, and, whenever necessary, an aggressive bread-and-butter liberalism in behalf of the lower and lower-middle income groups in both city and country.[13] Most of them are either mildly irritated or visibly outraged by the behavior of the Southerners in Congress. At the same time almost every Southern Democrat with whom I have talked insists that his state will not be forced one step faster toward desegregation than it chooses to move (if it chooses to move at all) and wonders out loud how long the ancient alliance will hold together. Well over half of them, in addition, express social and economic views indistinguishable from those of a Taft Republican in Shaker Heights or Sheboygan. As Fred Astaire puts it, "Something's got to give."

Three courses have been predicted or recommended for the Southern Democrats: (1) to form some kind of third party—the "real" Democracy—that would continue to govern each Southern state as it is presently governed, hold the balance of power in the electoral college, and make the best bargains it can with the most willing party of the moment in Congress; (2) to follow the path staked out in the presidential elections of 1952 and 1956 and divide along rough lines of class, interest, and principle into a genuine two-party pattern, first in states like Texas, Virginia, and Florida, eventually even in South Carolina and Mississippi; and (3) to hold on as long as possible in the present situation, certainly until the Northern Democrats force a final disruption by eliminating both the filibuster and the seniority rule, which they may never be able or willing to do. This course, incidentally, does not call for a perfect show of loyalty to the party. A little dabbling in walkouts from the convention, in presidential Republicanism, or in unpledged slates of electors would be permitted—but not too much.

As both a birthright and convinced Yankee, I am reluctant to predict which one of these courses the South will finally take. More than that, there seem to me to be immense obstacles strewn along all three of them. As to the first course, it defies every rule of American politics and assumes the existence of a massive unanimity of purpose in the South, a unanimity that might well perish at the second if not the first twisting. As to the second, it would be a much harder blow to "the Southern way of life" than token integration in a scatter of schools or the registration of another half-million Negroes or even the organization of the workers at Burlington Mills. It is not just the Republican party from which the courthouse politicians of the South shy away. That old problem could well be solved by a nationwide change of name, say, from Republican to Constitutional. (If Paris was "worth a mass" to Henry IV, the South might be worth a second baptism to the Republicans.) It is the notion of any kind of developed two-party politics that gives them nightmares. And even if the conservative half of the South could choke down its memories, vested interests, and fears and hold out its hands to the Republicans, would not many Republicans, men with names like Javits and Rockefeller and Judd and even Nixon,[14] find it impossible to grasp them firmly? A Republican (or Constitutional) party that made room for Senators Byrd and Eastland might find itself gutted by wholesale desertion,* and the "modern" wing of the party could be expected to put up a stiff fight against any such development.

---

* Then, again, it might not—not if predictions of a hardening of race lines in the North, as well as in the South, come true in the next decade. My own feeling is that such a hardening is not likely to develop to a sufficient degree to revolutionize the present minority-conscious pattern of Northern politics. This may be wishful thinking.

Yet the third course (which is to "roll with the punch" and stay with the party) also cannot be followed forever, as I trust I have already made clear. Surely the South of the year 2000 will have been forced to abandon its traditional patterns of political allegiance and organization. Surely it will have come to some modus vivendi on the race problem with the rest of the nation that will permit or even force the Southern states to follow the rest of the Union toward a more national politics. I am not certain when or how this transition from tradition to reality will take place in Southern politics, but I have a feeling that it will come roughly a generation from now, that it will be triggered by a violent break in the old Democracy forced by an aggressive President and the Northern liberals in Congress (and aided, in various honest and devious ways, by the Republicans), and that it will be far more swift than most people would now expect. What form this new reality will take I simply cannot say. The only thing of which I am certain is that it will serve the legitimate interests of Negroes in both the South and the North in at least a modest degree, or it, too, will crumble under pressure for yet another solution.

So much for prediction, for talk of what is likely to happen to the American political system. Now for prescription, for talk of what ought to happen. We should begin, I suppose, by reeling off a long list of criticisms of our present system, for there is not much point in prescribing changes in one that is constructed sensibly and functioning properly. But the words we would have to use—confusion, timidity, self-interest, corruption, dishonesty, oligarchy, apathy, irresponsibility, vulgarity—are so familiar to persons with even a passing interest in our politics that I must beg to be excused from what could only be an exercise in boredom.

More than that, we would find ourselves talking not of what was wrong with American parties but with the American

people, and, although that might be useful and amusing, it is a
subject for another book. In any case most criticisms of our
politics that I have listened to over the years, like most criticisms of Congress, television, high schools, Hollywood, college football, and newspapers, are first of all judgments on
the values and folkways of big, bourgeois democracy. Consider, for example, the strictures leveled at that noisy, plebeian,
maudlin, commercialized institution, the national party convention. Are these not at bottom denunciations of the noisy,
plebeian, maudlin, commercialized civilization within which it
operates? Must we not concede that the convention reflects
the values of the civilization because it is in fact so democratic
in character and purpose? Can we expect to reform the one
without first reforming the other? These questions, I think,
answer themselves, and we are therefore left to deal with the
parties as expressions of real values and instruments of real
purposes in a real country. If we are to criticize them at all
fairly and meaningfully, we must do it within the limits of
the real, and thus keep our prescriptions for improvement
within the limits of the possible.

If I may sum up a vast amount of effective, constructive
writing in five pregnant words, what our politics is said to
need by the best of its critics is more principle, clarity, discipline, responsibility, and enthusiasm. We can have much more
of all these Good Things, the critics insist, without disturbing
a single cherished value or time-tested procedure of American
democracy. They will come to us, as they should come, through
an act of collective will on our part. We will decide in time
that they are good, then move to convince our politicians that
it is only a question of putting new stress on old values and new
life in old procedures. Since our politicians live to be convinced,
it is for us alone to decide whether our politics is to be improved.

By more *principle*, the critics mean, of course, that we have
submitted too long to the tyranny of interests (whether vested
or merely hoped for) over the composition and operation of

our parties. It is time we caught up with at least the Canadians and British by injecting a modest dose of ideology (in the good sense of that word) into the political process. The parties, it is argued, will never function properly and thus deserve our respect until they stand for something more than the flag, home, mother, virtue, liberty, and progress—in a word, for victory. They have lived too smugly aloof from the thrust of ideas. The conservatism of the one has been entirely visceral, the liberalism of the other has been a mockery of the idealism of Jefferson and Wilson. What we need from both is a little less group diplomacy and a few more ideas about the American future.

This upsurge of principle will not be of much service to the American electorate if the ideas of the parties clash at only a few points. The parties should not merely stand for something, but for something different. There must be a *clarity* to the line that separates the Democrats from the Republicans. In E. E. Schattschneider's words, "The criticism most justly made of American major parties is not that they exhibit a tendency to be alike but rather that the moderate though significant differences between them are often too confused and ill defined to be readily understood." [15] The unwritten laws of American politics command that the differences between the parties be relatively few and modest, but it does not follow that these differences must also be obscure. Let the parties compete for the millions of Americans in the "vital center" by offering alternatives that do not wrench our minds too violently in one direction or the other, but let them also offer us alternatives that can be clearly grasped. So runs the argument for more principle and clarity in our politics.

I find this argument compelling. As a dogged admirer of the American political system, I would be most reluctant to have it overhauled boldly or tampered with carelessly in pursuit of the proposition that the parties should have ideas and the ideas should have consequences. Yet I cannot see that a sustained effort by the leaders of both parties to formulate more consistent programs based on more sharply defined principles, and to clarify the differences between one program and the other, would corrupt the solid virtues of that system in any way. Let the Democratic Advisory Council flourish and be taken up by the leaders of the party in Congress. Let the Republican Committee on Program and Progress be made a permanent adjunct of the National Committee. And let each send forth a continuing series of reports that seek to make clear just what the party stands for. Let it also, in words more moderate and elevated than those used in the spiteful, sputtering, meaningless debate carried on over the years between the chairmen of the national committees, make clear its own version of how it differs from the other.

Those differences must boil down in the end to a modest but meaningful confrontation of liberalism and conservatism. The confrontation already exists more sharply than most people seem to realize, as I tried to show in Chapter IV, and it is largely a question now of convincing our politicians, not so much to undertake the conscious realignment of which impatient men on both the left and right have spoken in recent years, but to be honest and open about what becomes more of a reality with each passing year. We can all sympathize with Governor Dewey's rejection in 1950 of the advice of "impractical theorists" who

want to drive all moderates and liberals out of the Republican party and then have the remainder join forces with the conservative groups of the South. Then they would have everything neatly arranged, indeed. The Democratic party would be the liberal-to-radical party. The Republican party would be the conservative-to-reactionary party.

The results would be neatly arranged, too. The Republicans would lose every election and the Democrats would win every election.[16]

Yet I wonder if he would not reconsider his views in 1960, a year in which the Conservative party in Great Britain has just

become the first in history to win three general elections in a
row and the Progressive Conservatives in Canada hold a 4 to 1
margin over the Liberals in Parliament. No one, so far as I
know, has suggested seriously that *all* "moderates and liberals"
should abandon the Republicans, that the sentiments of the reactionary South should govern the operations of the purged
party, and that it should stand obdurately against every form
of social progress. Certainly no one expects an American party
to label itself "Conservative," to ignore the vital center, or to
surrender the two ancient rights of political conservatism: to
accept, consolidate, administer, and eventually crow over the
reforms first enacted by its progressive adversaries—all this,
of course, after a decent interval; * and occasionally to surprise
liberalism with a reform of its own—to honor Disraeli, as it
were, rather than Stanley Baldwin. One can expect that in
matters like taxation, government spending, fiscal policy, regulation of labor and industry, aid to underdeveloped countries,
subsidies to agriculture, and benefits to the underprivileged, a
party more conservative than liberal, having its center of gravity
in the business community, and a party more liberal than conservative, having its center of gravity in the lower and lower-
middle classes, could contest for the stakes of power on a
fairly equal basis. They could, moreover, give us the range of
political choice—not too broad but broader than we have had
—we need and deserve as citizens of a country that has some
large problems to solve. Most of us do not want more principle
and clarity in our two-party system at the expense of the precious national and social unity to which the parties have been
major contributors. Still, we may already be well launched on
the way to a more clear-cut system, and I fail to detect any
new rips in the social fabric that have been caused by the pull-

---

* If the past is any evidence, the Republican party's platform of 1984
will proclaim that socialized medicine—jammed through by the Democrats and its own mavericks in 1973—ranks with apple pie and the
seventh-inning stretch as "a precious ingredient of the American Way
of Life."

ing and hauling of the parties. Indeed, I am confident that we can have it both ways: a party system that continues to work in its strange, offhanded way for unity of Americans of every section, class, and race and yet gives them a sharper choice of alternatives than it has given in the past.

That sharper choice will have to be reflected in a keener show of *discipline* in the two houses of Congress, say the critics of our present flabby system, or all our efforts to have a politics of at least modest principle and perceptible clarity will come to nothing. The Democratic Advisory Council and the Republican Committee on Program and Progress will swat at each other with pillows stuffed with platitudes, the mavericks in Congress will continue to pay nothing in the coin of loyalty for the privilege of wearing a party's badge, and the air will continue to be filled with pleas of professors, journalists, and just plain voters for "parties that stand for something different." We must have a more developed party consciousness among our legislators, more bite to the sanctions that can be imposed by the leadership upon recalcitrants, more protection for the man who defies a local interest or national pressure group to support his party's stand on a crucial issue, more respect in our folkways for the legislator who attempts to make good on the party's specific promises.

Discipline, of course, is only a means to a higher end, and that end—itself a means to an even higher end—is a party system that displays a genuine measure of *responsibility*. This is "the blessed word Mesopotamia" of all critics of American politics. This is the quality, we are told, that must be strengthened where it exists already in our system and introduced where it does not, lest we go on wallowing forever in the mire of a politics that exalts compromise and independence and deflates achievement and accountability, that raises up majorities to win great victories and then do almost nothing with them, that encourages the parties to behave like the Wizard of Oz and make grand promises they cannot keep.

The campaign for more responsible parties was launched a full three generations ago by a youthful Woodrow Wilson, and it continues unabated to this day. It reached a notable peak, at least in the academic world, in 1950, when the Committee on Political Parties of the American Political Science Association, under the leadership of E. E. Schattschneider, issued a thoughtful report entitled *Toward a More Responsible Two-Party System.*[17] The essence of the Committee's case is caught in these excerpts:

An effective party system requires, first, that the parties are able to bring forth programs to which they commit themselves and, second, that the parties possess sufficient internal cohesion to carry out these programs. In such a system, the party program becomes the work program of the party, so recognized by the party leaders in and out of the government, by the party body as a whole, and by the public. . . .

Party responsibility means the responsibility of both parties to the general public, as enforced in elections.

Responsibility of the party in power centers on the conduct of the government, usually in terms of policies. The party in power has a responsibility, broadly defined, for the general management of the government, for its manner of getting results, for the results achieved, for the consequences of inaction as well as action, for the intended and unintended outcome of its conduct of public affairs, for all that it plans to do, for all that it might have foreseen, for the leadership it provides, for the acts of all of its agents, and for what it says as well as for what it does.

Party responsibility includes the responsibility of the opposition party, also broadly defined, for the conduct of its opposition, for the management of public discussion, for the development of alternative policies and programs, for the bipartisan policies which it supports, for its failures and successes in developing the issues of public policy, and for its leadership of public opinion.[18]

From these premises the committee took off on a flight to London if not to Utopia, propelling their cargo of hopes along with a burst of suggestions, some precise and some vague, about the size and timing of national conventions, the creation of party councils, the stimulation of regional (as opposed to state and local) organizations, the formulation of more positive platforms, the tightening of leadership and organization in Congress, the restriction of the free play of the filibuster and the seniority rule, the encouragement of closed primaries, and the overhauling of the presidential electoral system.

I will spare my readers the endless details of the debate that followed hard upon the publication of this report and confine myself to two observations: First, the committee underestimated the amount of cohesion and responsibility that already exists in our government and framed too many of its proposals in an inspirational rather than institutional form. Second, many critics of the committee overestimated the amount of unwonted change that would supposedly take place in our political system if its plan of action were carried through and gave the report small credit for its modesty and moderation. In general, the committee did an able, conscientious job of pointing out the road that we may yet travel to more disciplined and responsible parties, and I would recommend it, if not as a blueprint certainly as a string of guideposts, to all who are interested in moving toward stronger party government.

My own view is that we could indeed use another three tablespoons of discipline and five pinches of responsibility in the glorious stew of American politics, but that we should halt after each addition and taste the stew carefully to be sure that it was not losing its bland but wholesome flavor of compromise, tolerance, and unity. Our basic commitment as a people, Austin Ranney points out, is to a constitutional pattern that "inhibits unlimited majority-rule" and thus calls for loose-jointed parties.[19] Until that commitment shifts radically toward the notion of dynamic, majoritarian government, which we dare not let it do so long as our society retains so much "civil-war potential," we would do well to cherish our present parties and work only gingerly for their improvement. Yet work we should—and with the hope of genuine results. Again I may be accused of seeking to have the best of both possible worlds, the present world of Lyndon Johnson and the future world of E. E. Schattschneider, but I do agree with the latter that the capacity of our system to produce and support responsible parties without damage to the American consensus is perhaps larger than we have hitherto recognized. In any case these are some of the modest steps we might consider taking: more active and efficient national party organizations, more assertive and at the same time protective leaders in Congress, more talk about responsibility to the national electorate, a seniority rule in Congress that is modified in the interest of party cohesion,* a four-year term for the House of Representatives (to be elected simultaneously with the President), machinery for open and consistent interchange between the President and the parties in Congress, and even perhaps (by constitutional amendment) a four-year term in the Senate for the candidate polling the second highest vote for the Presidency. (Why *not* try to make the Titular Leader a real one?)

For reasons that I have outlined in another place, I am not in favor at present of tampering with our time-tested system of electing the President,[21] whether in the interest of an allegedly more just and accurate measurement of popular sentiment or an allegedly more clear-cut and responsible two-party system. The progressive character of the Presidency might be undercut by the elimination of the general-ticket system, and that is a change we might live to regret. When Congress is no longer elected on a system gerrymandered in favor of the rural

---

* To my way of thinking, this is the first place to experiment gingerly. I recognize the merits of the present system, which saves Congress an infinite amount of energy, intrigue, and rancor (and keeps the President out of its hair), but I also think that eight Southern chairmen out of ten in the key committees of the Senate is about five too many. Surely the American political genius has an answer to this nagging problem.[20]

interests, it may be proper to elect the President on a system no longer gerrymandered in favor of the urban interests. Until then we would do well to keep the present balance between the two great branches of our government, comforting ourselves with the thought that one good gerrymander deserves another.[22]

To retreat for a moment from prescription to prediction, I think we need have little fear that any progress we make toward responsible party government will change the familiar pattern of American politics to any pronounced degree. What all this talk of responsibility comes down to is a hope—a hope, incidentally, that springs most naturally in liberal breasts—that each of our parties will present a more united front to the country in congressional elections and that successful candidates will value considerations of party higher than those of constituency in making their decisions in Congress. Any trend in this direction will certainly move only glacially against the vast accumulation of habits, values, and institutions that support our present pattern of politics. Even if these were to disintegrate and form themselves into a different pattern, we would still be dealing with a country of common principles and varied interests. The blessed fact of the American consensus forces the parties to share many of the same ideas; the blessed fact of American diversity forces them to be selective about the ideas they may wish to emphasize at any one time or in any one place. As Julius Turner argued cogently, "Only a Democrat who rejects a part of the Fair Deal can carry Kansas, and only a Republican who moderates the Republican platform can carry Massachusetts." [23] This situation may trouble those who like to have their politics neatly arranged, but it is still the price as well as the product of union.

All in all, the most we can hope for in the next few decades is a small reduction of the many mansions that stand in the house of each party and a somewhat larger increase in party loyalty and discipline in Congress. What we *can* hope for, I am bound to add, we *should* hope for.

The final injection prescribed by critics for the toning-up of our flabby politics is a large dose of *enthusiasm*. Madison Avenue, which cannot suffer apathy gladly, is perhaps more concerned with the pattern of casual participation and massive nonvoting I described in Chapter I than are the academic exponents of party responsibility, but almost everyone is agreed that we should do better—and could do better if we tried—as citizens of a great and proud democracy. A 45 per cent turnout in congressional elections, a 60 per cent in presidential elections, and a refusal of more than 10 per cent to be politically engaged—is this the best response Americans can make to the challenge of democracy in these momentous years?

I feel compelled to answer that it probably is, and that we are not going to do appreciably better over the next few elections. No one of the major causes for our political inertia—the burdens and disabilities that beset would-be voters, the soporific effects of our peculiar two-party system, the limited commitment we have to politics and almost unlimited faith we have in our democracy—is likely to be any less compelling in the next generation. Despite the pleas of the Get-out-the-Vote-ers, we will continue to vote and not vote, to contribute and not contribute, to participate and not participate in the proportions of the past decade. Idaho will turn out close to 80 per cent of its electorate every four years; Mississippi will plow along dismally with a showing one-fourth as good. Most of the money that keeps our parties alive will come from relatively few sources; most of those people who support one party or the other at the polls will feel no compulsion to go beyond mere support and to work for the party either in season or out. The politics of American democracy will continue to be noted for the coolness with which most citizens watch it or play it. In the heat of a national campaign we may seem anything but cool, yet as Henry Jones Ford remarked many years ago, "The truth is that a remarkable nonchalance underlies the sound and fury of partisan politics." [24]

Although this may seem heretical to many well-meaning Americans, I think we should be more content with the nonchalance we have hitherto demonstrated, especially as it displays itself in the turnout in national elections. It would be heartening to have all disabilities and difficulties removed so that the nationwide figure could rise to its apparently natural level of 72 to 78 per cent,[25] but I see no point in pushing furiously for a large turnout simply for the sake of a large turnout. This, in my opinion, is exactly what the Get-out-the-Voters have been doing, and I have yet to learn how it would make any practical difference to the American future whether the turnout in the next election were 50, 60, 70, 80, or 90 per cent. As free men we all ought to vote, or have legitimate, principled reasons for not voting; but as free men we all ought to do a lot of things more faithfully and virtuously than we do them at present, and voting may stand about tenth in the list of the priorities of improved social behavior for millions of Americans.

I am not writing in defense of apathy. That defense has already been made with wit and persuasion by a number of scholars and journalists more concerned than I to bait or belabor the merchants of mass democracy.[26] I want only to point to three things generally overlooked in the quadrennial hue and cry over our performance as an electorate: First, what men call "apathy" has many faces, not all of them evil, not all of them apathetic. A collective indifference to politics can be a major bulwark against extremism and autocracy;[27] individual withdrawal may be as meaningful and democratic an act for one man as a zealous vote is for another. For these and other reasons, it is yet to be proved that a nation's voting record is a reliable indication of the health of its democracy. "A realistic view of the behavior of democracies," Francis Wilson writes, "leads one toward the belief that there is no danger in the continued absence of a large number of the legally established electorate from the voting booth." [28] Second, a sudden increase in electoral activity may be a sign of danger rather than of improved health in a constitutional democracy. There is considerable evidence to support S. M. Lipset's observation that a high level of participation is an imperative for leaders who seek to disrupt or revolutionize a country's social system.[29] If America ever "goes to hell" in a national election, it will be one, I suspect, in which a very high turnout is marked up. This is not an argument against efforts to improve our present record; it is merely a way of saying that we should expect no great gains for democracy from a sizable improvement over the years, indeed, that we should not be surprised if a harsher politics comes with it. Third, our future rests on the quality of our votes (and of our participation) rather than on the quantity. What we need is not more voters, but more good voters, men and women who are intelligent, alert, informed, understanding, and reasonable. If we can produce such men and women in ever larger numbers, we need have no fear of losing our freedom by way of the ballot box. If we cannot, the most nearly perfect voting record in the world will be no better than a measure of the passion of the times.*

In this regard, I think it only fair to remind my readers that

---

* Those who concentrate on quantity at the expense of quality may wish to be reminded of the vote in California for State Superintendent of Public Instruction in 1950, in which, in a nonpartisan election, Roy E. Simpson (listed as "incumbent") received 1,771,245 votes to 605,393 for Bernadette Doyle (listed as "educator and organizer"). Miss Doyle's real occupation, stated openly at the time of her filing and broadcast in every newspaper for weeks on end, was "chairman and education director of the Communist Party of San Diego." Was a careless or uninformed vote for Miss Doyle a better vote than no vote at all? I would rather have known and followed the example of the tens of thousands of citizens of Sao Paulo, Brazil, who showed their opinion of conditions prevalent in 1959 by electing a rhinoceros (also female) to the city council.

uneducated people vote in fewer numbers than do educated and Democrats in fewer numbers than do Republicans. Let us be perfectly frank about the probable results of a jump from 62 to, let us say, 78 per cent in the nationwide turnout for a presidential election. The quality of the electorate would decline, and with it the level of the campaign; the Democrats would win their biggest victory in history; the enthusiasm of many well-meaning people for getting out the vote would grow cold and die. This is not to be construed as advice to one party or the other, but to be taken simply as an observation grounded on some of the hard facts of political life in the United States. One of those facts, which has been demonstrated again and again in elections, is that the Democrats must work harder than the Republicans to turn out their own habitual and potential voters. Since they usually do, they usually win. If I were a Republican party worker, I would shun the broad if patriotic advice of the American Heritage Foundation and work to get out only my own habitual and potential voters.

When all our hopes for the reform of American politics have been laid out and picked over, the stubborn fact remains that the pattern we have known in the recent past is likely to persist in the foreseeable future. Even the breakup of the Solid South is not going to alter the main features of that pattern. They are now so firmly rooted in the values, institutions, and circumstances of the American people that nothing short of a profound revolution in our way of life, whether generated from within or imposed from without, would wrench them loose. We may well come in time to a sharper line of ideological division between the two parties, to a new age of Republican ascendancy, to real two-party competition in every state of the Union, even to stronger party government in Congress, yet these would only be shifts in emphasis within the present pattern of politics. That pattern strikes me as durable.

It also strikes me as admirable, which is to say that the durability of the politics of American democracy should be a cause of modest rejoicing rather than of gnawing frustration.[30] It may be that such a politics will have no place in the fanciful world of 2060—painless, antiseptic, automatic, and abundant— we have been promised by our seers, but for the time being it can serve the peculiar needs of American democracy better than can any other politics we have been pressed to adopt. It is said that our present problems of defense and diplomacy will never be solved by a politics of compromise, but that is to say that they will never be solved by constitutional democracy. Should we therefore abandon our democracy, and, if so, what system of decision making and governing should we adopt in its place? It is said that our mounting problems of health, welfare, education, transportation, and recreation will call for more determined solutions than those our politics is geared to produce, but that is to say that we have not yet felt enough drag on our progress to shift the gears one notch higher. Should we therefore scrap the whole machine, and, if so, what means of controlling the struggle for power should we experiment with next?

The severe critics of our party system and doubters of its "capacity to meet the challenge of the times" overlook three persistent facts about the politics of American democracy. First, it is designed to check but not to suppress the rule of the majority. When that majority, in Charles A. Beard's celebrated phrase, shows itself to be "persistent and undoubted," it will break through the restraints of the party system just as it breaks through those of the Constitution. The persistent and undoubted majority in favor of most of the reforms and programs that now seem to be hamstrung by the party system has simply not emerged. Second, the politics of American democracy, indeed of any constitutional democracy, does not require that every majority decision be first of all a party decision. Partisanship must have a large place in the process of making public decisions, yet so, too, when the situation permits or demands it, must bipartisanship and nonpartisanship. There is nothing about the form or spirit of responsible party government that demands a clear division on every issue, or that, conversely, forbids the continued existence of sectional or economic blocs. Surely there are matters, such as appropriations for existing commitments, in which sharply divided parties—one of which would always be gunning viciously for the President—would be less efficient instruments of the public business. Surely there are questions, such as disarmament or the importance of reaching into outer space, to which partisan considerations are likely to bring only ill-digested answers. All partisanship must be political, but not all politics must be partisan.[31] In the American system, I repeat, there are many ways to form and express majority sentiment, and even the best friends of parties would not presume to assert a monopoly of this process.

Finally, it must be recognized that free government reaches only part of the way into the lives of the people who support it. There are things it cannot do by right or might or nature, and we must remember not to expect too much of it. Remembering that, we will also remember not to expect too much of politics, which exists, after all, as an adjunct of government. Politics is only one of several mighty forces that made America what it is today; it is only one of the forces that will make America what it is in 1984 or 2000 or 2060.

Let us ask more of our politics than we have hitherto received, but let us not make the mistake of asking more than it can give. Our party system will continue to serve us well as long as we keep the old definition firmly in mind: Politics is the art of the possible. Whatever America finds necessary to do in the years to come, the politics of American democracy will surely make possible.

Notes

CHAPTER I

1. Austin Ranney and Willmoore Kendall, *Democracy and the American Party System* (New York, 1956), 454.

2. V. O. Key, *Politics, Parties, and Pressure Groups* (New York, 1958), chap. 10 and works cited at p. 282. A major history and analysis of American third parties is desperately needed.

3. John D. Hicks, *The Populist Revolt* (Minneapolis, 1931).

4. *Politics, Parties, and Pressure Groups*, 307.

5. *The Revolt of the Moderates* (New York, 1956), 204.

6. *Democracy and the American Party System*, 157–166. V. O. Key, *American State Politics* (New York, 1956), is an insightful introduction to this only vaguely understood area of American political life.

7. William Goodman, *The Two-Party System in the United States* (Princeton, 1956), 29–39.

8. *Political Parties* (London, 1954), 215.

9. Neil A. McDonald, *The Study of Political Parties* (Garden City, 1955), 34.

10. The strongest case for the influence of the single-member district is made by F. A. Hermens, *Democracy or Anarchy?* (Notre Dame, 1941), and E. E. Schattschneider, *Party Government* (New York, 1942), chap. 5.

11. Belle Zeller and Hugh A. Bone, "The Repeal of P. R. in New York City—Ten Years in Retrospect," *American Political Science Review* (hereafter cited as *APSR*), XLII (1948), 1127.

12. *Our Two-Party System* (University, Miss., 1951), 1.

13. "Is Our Two-Party System 'Natural'?" *Annals*, CCLIX (1948), 1, 9.

14. *Politics, Parties, and Pressure Groups*, 347.

15. *Party Government*, 163.

16. *Toward a More Responsible Two-Party System* (New York, 1950), 40–41, a document produced by the Committee on Political Parties of the American Political Science Association under the chairmanship of E. E. Schattschneider, hereafter cited as *APSA Report*.

17. *New York Times*, Oct. 12, 1956.

18. *Democracy and the American Party System*, 264.

19. The literature of bossism is vast and colorful. See P. H. Odegard and E. A. Helms, *American Politics* (New York, 1947), chaps. 14–15, and the many works there cited; Harold Zink, *City Bosses in the United States* (Durham, N.C., 1930); J. T. Salter, *Boss Rule* (New York, 1935), which deals with the second rank of bosses; Frank R. Kent, *The Great Game of Politics* (Buffalo, 1959), which was first published in 1923 and still makes delightful reading.

20. *The Condition of Our National Political Parties* (New York, 1959), 7.

21. Malcolm E. Jewell, "Party Voting in American State Legislatures," *APSR*, XLIX (1955), 773.

22. David B. Truman, "The State Delegations and the Structure of Party Voting in the United States House of Representatives," *APSR*, L (1956), 1023; James M. Burns, *Congress on Trial* (New York, 1949), 35.

23. *Party and Constituency* (Baltimore, 1952), 28.

24. *Party Government*, 130–132, by permission of the publisher, Rinehart and Company. Burns and Schattschneider both overstate their case, as I hope to make clear in Chapter IV.

25. C. A. Berdahl, "Some Notes on Party Membership in Congress," *APSR*, XLIII (1949), 309, 494.

26. *The American Federal Government* (New York, 1959), 148.

27. George Grassmuck, *Sectional Biases in Congress on Foreign Policy* (Baltimore, 1951), 13–14, 54–55, 171–172; H. B. Westerfield, *Foreign Policy and Party Politics* (New Haven, 1955).

28. Schattschneider, *Party Government*, chap. 8; Key, *Politics, Parties, and Pressure Groups*, chaps. 2–6, and works cited at p. 23. The pioneering study of the group nature of American politics was Arthur F. Bentley's *The Process of Government* (1908; Evanston, Ill., 1949). Bentley has been brought up to date by David B. Truman, *The Governmental Process* (New York, 1951). The best short statement of this approach is Earl Latham, "The Group Basis of Politics: Notes for a Theory," *APSR*, XLVI (1952), 376.

29. *APSA Report*, 4.

30. Key, *Politics, Parties, and Pressure Groups*, 172.

31. M. Ostrogorski, *Democracy and the Organization of Political Parties* (New York, 1908), II, 185.

32. For a useful introduction to the whole question of political behavior in the United States, see Robert E. Lane, *Political Life* (Glencoe, Ill., 1959), esp. pts. 2–3.

33. "Political Activity of American Citizens," *APSR*, XLIV (1950), 872.

34. Angus Campbell, Gerald Gurin, and W. E. Miller, *The Voter Decides* (Evanston, Ill., 1954), 39–40.

35. Key, *Politics, Parties, and Pressure Groups*, chap. 18.

36. *Political Parties* (London, 1915), pt. 6.

37. A. Campbell and W. E. Miller, "The Motivational Basis of Straight and Split Ticket Voting," *APSR*, LI (1957), 293.

38. S. J. Eldersveld, "The Independent Vote," *APSR*, XLVI (1952), 732, and studies cited in notes 1–14.

39. "Are the Republicans Through?" *Saturday Evening Post*, Feb. 14, 1959.

40. For a review of the best available statistics, which I have checked independently with the aid of *Historical Statistics of the United States, 1789–1945* (Washington, 1941), old editions of *The World Almanac*, publications of the American Heritage Foundation, and other lists, see Lane, *Political Life*, 21, and works there cited. I have found *The Gallup Political Almanac* (1952) and Richard Scammon's series *America Votes* (1956, 1958) especially useful compilations of voting statistics.

41. See D. O. McGovney, *The American Suffrage Medley* (Chicago, 1949), chap. 5, on "educational qualifications for voting."

42. Louis Harris, *Is There a Republican Majority?* (New York, 1954), 107–109.

43. Campbell *et al.*, *The Voter Decides*, 70–73; Harris, *Is There a Republican Majority?* 16–17. For the evidence in this matter, much of it drawn from Europe and corroborative of American experience, see H. S. Tingsten, *Political Behavior* (London, 1937); S. M. Lipset, *Political Man* (Glencoe, Ill., 1960), 182–186, and works cited at pp. 182–183n.

44. Howard R. Penniman, *Sait's American Parties and Elections* (New York, 1952), chap. 25; S. D. Albright, *The American Ballot* (Washington, 1942).

45. P. F. Lazarsfeld, B. Berelson, and Hazel Gaudet, *The People's Choice* (New York, 1944), 62; Lipset, *Political Man*, 203–216, and works there cited.

46. On the whole question of nonvoting and motivation, see Lipset, *Political Man*, chap. 6; Lane, *Political Life*; C. E. Merriam and H. F. Gosnell, *Non-Voting* (Chicago, 1924), a pioneering study; J. K. Pollock, *Voting Behavior* (Ann Arbor, 1939); David Riesman and Nathan Glazer, "Criteria for Political Apathy," in A. W. Gouldner, ed., *Studies in*

Leadership (New York, 1950), 505–559; G. M. Connelly and H. H. Field, "The Non-Voter—Who He Is, What He Thinks," *Public Opinion Quarterly* (hereafter cited as *POQ*), VIII (1944), 175; M. Rosenberg, "Some Determinants of Political Apathy," *POQ*, XVIII (1954–1955), 349; Lazarsfeld *et al.*, *The People's Choice*, 45–49; Campbell *et al.*, *The Voter Decides*, chaps. 3, 5; Bernard Berelson, Paul F. Lazarsfeld, and William McPhee, *Voting* (Chicago, 1954), 24–34; Louis Bean, *How to Predict Elections* (New York, 1948), chap. 5.

47. *The Lonely Crowd* (New Haven, 1950), 187.

48. *APSR*, XLIV (1950), 877, by permission of the American Political Science Association.

CHAPTER II

1. Goodman, *Two-Party System*, chap. 2.

2. Penniman, *Sait's American Parties and Elections*, pts. 4–5.

3. Joseph R. Starr, "The Legal Status of American Parties," *APSR*, XXXIV (1940), 439, 685.

4. *APSA Report*, 15.

5. Ranney and Kendall, *Democracy and the American Party System*, chap. 17; Key, *Politics, Parties, and Pressure Groups*, 715ff.

6. Belle Zeller, ed., *American State Legislatures* (New York, 1954), chap. 12; O. D. Weeks, "Politics in the Legislatures," *National Municipal Review*, XLI (1952), 80.

7. C. E. Merriam and H. F. Gosnell, *The American Party System* (New York, 1947), 433ff.

8. Quoted in Odegard and Helms, *American Politics*, 480.

9. Quoted in Robert C. Wood, *Suburbia* (Boston, 1959), 37.

10. *Human Nature in Politics* (Boston, 1909), 83.

11. *American Party System*, 435.

12. Roy F. Nichols, *The Disruption of American Democracy* (New York, 1948); W. E. Binkley, *American Political Parties* (New York, 1947), chaps. 8–9.

13. C. Vann Woodward, *Reunion and Reaction* (Boston, 1951); Paul H. Buck, *The Road to Reunion, 1865–1900* (Boston, 1937).

14. *Politics in America* (New York, 1954), 54, by permission of the publisher, Harper and Brothers.

15. *The Price of Union* (Boston, 1950), a bold statement of this thesis.

16. Ranney and Kendall, *Democracy and the American Party System*, chap. 20, pp. 507–513, an insightful and elaborate review of some of the points I have been making.

17. *Party Government*, 124. See generally Avery Leiserson, *Parties and Politics* (New York, 1958), chap. 3.

CHAPTER III

1. *Works* (Boston, 1851), X, 23.

2. Ranney and Kendall, *Democracy and the American Party System,* pt. 2, and books there cited, especially Ostrogorski, *Democracy and the Organization of Political Parties* I, 135ff., and II, 3ff.

3. Harris, *Is There a Republican Majority?* 5, 15, 219–220.

4. Angus Campbell and H. C. Cooper, *Group Differences in Attitudes and Votes* (Ann Arbor, 1956), 17, by permission of the Survey Research Center; Key, *Politics, Parties, and Pressure Groups,* 234.

5. Two general histories of American parties stand out above all others in scope and insight: Binkley, *American Political Parties,* and Agar, *The Price of Union.* Interesting treatments of each major party are Frank R. Kent, *The Democratic Party, A History* (New York, 1928), and Malcolm Moos, *The Republicans* (New York, 1956).

6. Noble E. Cunningham, Jr., *The Jeffersonian Republicans: The Formation of Party Organization, 1789–1801* (Chapel Hill, 1957), a refreshing study, from which I have learned much.

7. For new light on Jefferson's role, which was a good deal less creative than he is generally given credit for, see Cunningham, *Jeffersonian Republicans,* esp. 257–259; Joseph Charles, *The Origins of the American Party System* (Williamsburg, 1956), 74–90.

8. Cunningham, *Jeffersonian Republicans,* 21–23, 51–53, 67–88, 257–259.

9. R. V. Remini, *Martin Van Buren and the Making of the Democratic Party* (New York, 1959), chap. 10. For light on the elections of 1828–1836, see R. P. McCormick, "New Perspectives on Jacksonian Politics," *American Historical Review,* LXV (1960), 288. The election of 1840 was apparently the first truly popular presidential canvass in our history.

10. *Politics in America,* 50.

11. Burton J. Hendrick, *Lincoln's War Cabinet* (Boston, 1946).

12. *The Future of American Politics* (New York, 1956), chaps. 10–11. For a case study of the part that Al Smith played in building the Democratic majority, see J. J. Huthmacher, *Massachusetts People and Politics* (Cambridge, 1959), esp. chap. 6.

13. *Politics, Parties, and Pressure Groups,* 251.

14. The weaknesses of the minority party in one-party states are discussed in Warren Miller, "One-Party Politics and the Voter," *APSR,* L (1956), 707.

15. *APSA Report,* 33. The first observer to take careful note of this trend was Arthur N. Holcombe in his *New Party Politics* (New York, 1933), in which he spoke perceptively of the changes that had taken place since the publication of his *The Political Parties of Today* (New York, 1924). Holcombe's most recent thoughts on our politics are in his

Our More Perfect Union (Cambridge, 1950), chaps. 4–5. For a review of the influence of sectionalism and a useful bibliography, see Goodman, *Two-Party System,* chap. 14.

16. Harold F. Gosnell, *Grass Roots Politics* (Washington, 1942), gives evidence gathered in six key states. Russel B. Nye, *Midwestern Progressive Politics* (East Lansing, 1959), is a case study of a persistent urge in an enduring section.

17. For the Northern-Southern New England break, see Duane Lockard, *New England State Politics* (Princeton, 1959).

18. Lubell, *Future of American Politics,* 30.

19. Key, *American State Politics,* 230–236.

20. Wood, *Suburbia,* esp. chap. 5.

21. *Revolt of the Moderates,* 112. This table and also Tables 4–7 are quoted by permission of the publisher, Harper and Brothers.

22. Wood, *Suburbia,* 63.

23. *Revolt of the Moderates,* 113.

24. *The American Commonwealth,* 2nd ed. (New York, 1891), II, 30–31. For evidence of the influence of class throughout American political history, see Lipset, *Political Man,* chap. 9.

25. *American Life: Dream and Reality* (Chicago, 1953), chap. 3, and references 1, 7, and 12 at pp. 239–241.

26. Heinz Eulau, "Perceptions of Class and Party in Voting Behavior: 1952," *APSR,* XLIX (1955), 364; Berelson *et al., Voting,* chap. 4.

27. *National Municipal Review,* VI (1917), 204.

28. *Revolt of the Moderates,* 184.

29. *Revolt of the Moderates,* 186.

30. *Revolt of the Moderates,* 283. See also the evidence gathered by James Prothro, *et al.,* "Two-Party Voting in the South: Class vs. Party Identification," *APSR,* LII (1958), 130.

31. Key, *Politics, Parties, and Pressure Groups,* 543, which was based directly on the report of the Gore Committee (Subcommittee on Privileges and Elections of the Senate Committee on Rules and Administration, 1956).

32. "Corporations Make Politics Their Business," *Fortune,* December, 1959; Osborn Elliott, *Men at the Top* (New York, 1959), chap. 14; Andrew Hacker, "Politics and the Corporation," an occasional pamphlet issued by the Fund for the Republic (1958), which has a useful bibliography.

33. Harris, *Is There a Republican Majority?* 140–151.

34. For evidence of the Democratic leanings of union workers, see Arthur Kornhauser *et al., When Labor Votes: A Study of Auto Workers* (New York, 1956); Harold L. Sheppard and Nicholas A. Masters, "The Political Attitudes and Preferences of Union Members: The Case of the Detroit Auto Workers," *APSR,* LIII (1959), 437, and works there cited.

35. *Future of American Politics,* 179.

36. Lubell, *Future of American Politics*, chap. 8, and *Revolt of the Moderates*, chap. 7.

37. Lubell, *Revolt of the Moderates*, 80.

38. Harris, *Is There a Republican Majority?* chap. 6; Brogan, *Politics in America*, chap. 3.

39. Harris, *Is There a Republican Majority?* 221.

40. W. Cohn, "The Politics of the Jews," in M. Sklare, ed., *The Jews: Social Patterns of an American Group* (Glencoe, Ill., 1958), 614–626; Lawrence H. Fuchs, *Political Behavior of American Jews* (Glencoe, Ill., 1956), and "American Jews and the Presidential Vote," *APSR*, XLIX (1955), 385.

41. *Political Man*, 289.

42. H. L. Moon, *Balance of Power* (New York, 1948); Harris, *Is There a Republican Majority?* 76–79, 152–160; Lubell, *Future of American Politics*, 100–109.

43. Harris, *Is There a Republican Majority?* 153.

44. Margaret Price, *The Negro and the Ballot in the South* (Atlanta, 1959), 8–10.

45. Campbell *et al.*, *The Voter Decides*, 70, 72, by permission of the publisher, Row, Peterson and Company.

46. Paul F. Lazarsfeld and Wagner Thielens, Jr., *The Academic Mind* (Glencoe, Ill., 1958), 14, 28, 401–402. See generally Lipset, *Political Man*, chap. 10.

47. Harris, *Is There a Republican Majority?* chap. 7.

48. Dayton McKean, *Party and Pressure Politics* (Boston, 1949), 101.

49. Goodman, *Two-Party System*, 288–289; Schattschneider, *Party Government*, 21; Lazarsfeld *et al.*, *The People's Choice*, xx; Campbell *et al.*, *The Voter Decides*, 98–100; H. H. Hyman, *Political Socialization* (Glencoe, Ill., 1959), chap. 4.

50. See the evidence on this point gathered by V. O. Key and Frank Munger in their study of Indiana politics in E. Burdick and A. J. Brodbeck, eds., *American Voting Behavior* (Glencoe, Ill., 1959), chap. 15.

CHAPTER IV

1. Bryce, *American Commonwealth*, II, 20.

2. *Republican Fact-Book* (Washington, 1948), 5.

3. *Forty Years of It* (New York, 1914), 27.

4. L. H. Chamberlain, *The President, Congress and Legislation* (New York, 1946), chap. 3.

5. Thanks to the *Congressional Quarterly Almanac*, an invaluable aid to students of American national politics, the "trudging" was really quite an enjoyable expedition.

6. Harris, *Is There a Republican Majority?* 41.

7. F. P. Dunne, *Mr. Dooley: Now and Forever* (Stanford, 1954), 165–166.

8. V. O. Key, *Southern Politics in State and Nation* (New York, 1949); Alexander Heard, *A Two-Party South?* (Chapel Hill, 1952); J. B. Shannon, *Towards a New Politics in the South* (Knoxville, 1949). Lipset, *Political Man*, chap. 11, is an interesting second look at the election of 1860 as the turning point for Southern politics.

9. Key, *Southern Politics*, 82, 277.

10. C. A. M. Ewing, *Primary Elections in the South* (Norman, Okla., 1953).

11. *Southern Politics*, 5, by permission of the publisher, Alfred A. Knopf.

12. The Republican split on foreign policy has been both sectional and ideological, as this table worked out by Samuel Lubell proves graphically:

Republican Isolationist Vote in Congress:
Per Cent "No" of Total Republican Votes

Region	Selective Service	Lend-Lease	Marshall Plan	Foreign-aid Bills			
				1952	1953	1954	1955
Midwest	98	97	47	76	70	69	65
East	70	68	4	24	13	13	19
Pacific	60	80	4	30	18	20	19
All Republicans	89	86	25	53	40	40	40

From *Revolt of the Moderates*, 98, by permission of the publisher, Harper and Brothers.

13. Gordon E. Baker, *Rural versus Urban Political Power* (Garden City, 1955), chap. 5.

14. George Goodwin, Jr., "The Seniority System in Congress," *APSR*, LIII (1959), 412. An interesting study of the "legislative parties" is David B. Truman, *The Congressional Party* (New York, 1959).

15. David Butler, "American Myths about British Parties," *Virginia Quarterly Review*, XXI (1955), 46.

16. Bailey, *Condition of our National Political Parties*, 22. For other evidence, less encouraging on this point, see the studies cited in Ranney and Kendall, *Democracy and the American Party System*, 477.

CHAPTER V

1. *Encyclopedia of the Social Sciences*, XI, 596.

2. The material in the next few pages is adapted (somewhat reluc-

tantly) from my book *The American Presidency* (2nd ed.; New York, 1960), 201–206, by permission of the publisher, Harcourt, Brace and Company. For an exhaustive case study of the politics of the nominating process, see Paul T. David *et al.*, *Presidential Nominating Politics*, 5 vols. (Baltimore, 1954), and for a compendium of knowledge about the convention, see David *et al.*, *The Politics of National Party Conventions* (Washington, 1960).

3. *Future of American Politics*, 21.

4. On Eisenhower's appeal to the Democrats, see Harris, *Is There a Republican Majority?* 45, 57–58, 171; H. Hyman and P. B. Sheatsley, "The Political Appeal of President Eisenhower," *POQ*, XVII (1953), 443.

5. W. E. Binkley, *The Man in the White House* (Baltimore, 1958), 97.

6. *APSA Report*, 20; Paul T. David, "The Changing Party Pattern," *Antioch Review*, XVI (1956), 333, 343–346.

7. Lazarsfeld *et al.*, *The People's Choice*.

8. S. P. Huntington, "A Revised Theory of American Party Politics," *APSR*, XLIV (1950), 669, 675–677.

9. For a slightly malicious but insightful presentation of this point of view, see Walter Prescott Webb, *An Honest Preface* (Boston, 1959), 78–97, on "How the Republican Party Lost Its Future."

10. *New York Times*, May 14, 1959.

11. *Revolt of the Moderates*, 213.

12. Key, *Southern Politics*, esp. chap. 31; Heard, *A Two-Party South?* esp. chap. 19; Lubell, *Future of American Politics*, chap. 6, and *Revolt of the Moderates*, chap. 8; Harris, *Is There a Republican Majority?* 79–81.

13. The best recent statement of the need for Democratic liberalism is Chester Bowles, *The Coming Political Breakthrough* (New York, 1959).

14. A strong statement of this kind of Republicanism is Arthur Larson's *A Republican Looks at His Party* (New York, 1956).

15. *Party Government*, 92–93.

16. *New York Times*, Feb. 9, 1950.

17. For introduction to the main points of debate and to the vast literature on this subject, see Ranney and Kendall, *Democracy and the American Party System*, 151–153, 384–385, 525–533; Ivan Hinderaker, *Party Politics* (New York, 1956), pt. 6. Ranney's *The Doctrine of Responsible Party Government* (Urbana, 1954), is much the best single treatment of the problem, but I would also recommend highly the critical rejoinders of Julius Turner, "Responsible Parties: A Dissent from the Floor," *APSR*, XLV (1951), 143; Murray Stedman and Herbert Sonthoff, "Party Responsibility—A Critical Inquiry," *Western Political Quarterly*, IV (1951), 546; William Goodman, "How Much Political Party Centralization Do We Want?" *Journal of Politics*, XIII (1951), 536; Norton E. Long, "Party Government and the United States," *Journal of Politics*, XIII (1951), 187; and the penetrating review by Stephen K. Bailey in his pamphlet *The Condition of Our National Political Parties*. Burns, *Con-*

gress on Trial, esp. chap. 11, makes a strong case for reform, which is made even more pointedly in his "Two-Party Stalemate," *Atlantic Monthly,* February, 1960.

18. *APSA Report,* 17–18, 22, by permission of the American Political Science Association. For Schattschneider's own ideas, see his *The Struggle for Party Government* (College Park, Md., 1948).

19. *Doctrine of Responsible Party Government,* 160, following A. Lawrence Lowell.

20. For wise words in defense of the present arrangement, see Stewart L. Udall, "A Defense of the Seniority System," *New York Times Magazine,* Jan. 13, 1957. For an excellent review of the whole subject, see Goodwin's article in *APSR,* LIII (1959), 412.

21. *The American Presidency,* 194–199.

22. On the discouraging extent of rural overrepresentation in Congress and the state legislatures, see Baker, *Rural versus Urban Political Power;* Richard L. Strout, "The Next Election Is Already Rigged," *Harper's,* November, 1959.

23. *APSR,* XLV (1951), 151.

24. *The Rise and Growth of American Politics* (New York, 1898), 304.

25. H. S. Commager, "Why Almost Half of Us Don't Vote," *New York Times Magazine,* Oct. 28, 1956.

26. Tingsten, *Political Behavior,* 225–226; Eric Larrabee, "Not the Number, but the Quality of Voters," *New York Times Magazine,* Sept. 28, 1952; D. H. Hogan, *Election and Representation* (Cork, 1945), 275ff.; Francis G. Wilson, "The Inactive Electorate and Social Revolution," *Southwestern Social Science Quarterly,* XVI (1936), 75, and "The Pragmatic Electorate," *APSR,* XXXIV (1930), 16; W. H. Morris Jones, "In Defence of Apathy," *Political Studies,* II (1954), 25; Lipset, *Political Man,* chap. 6.

27. David Riesman, *Individualism Reconsidered* (Glencoe, Ill., 1954), 414–425.

28. *Southwest Social Science Quarterly,* XVI (1936), 76.

29. *Political Man,* 180.

30. The most intelligent and persuasive defenses of our politics that I have read are Pendleton Herring, *The Politics of Democracy* (New York, 1940); Agar, *The Price of Union,* esp. chap. 35; Ranney and Kendall, *Democracy and the American Party System,* esp. chap. 22; Malcolm Moos, *Politics, Presidents and Coattails* (Baltimore, 1952), chap. 6; John Fischer, "Unwritten Rules of American Politics," *Harper's,* November, 1948.

31. For a review of the dangers of keen partisanship in foreign policy, see Westerfield, *Foreign Policy and Party Politics,* 5–16.

This book is based on a series of lectures given on the John L. Senior endowment at Cornell University in February and March, 1960. I am grateful to Andrew Hacker, Ruth P. Cogen, and Mary Crane Rossiter for their aid and comfort in bringing it to completion.

CLINTON ROSSITER

Ithaca, New York
March 31, 1960

Index